Criminal La

2012–2013

D0534961

Eighth edition published 2012
by Routledge
2 Park Square, Milton Park, Abingdon, Oxon OX14 4RN

Simultaneously published in the USA and Canada
by Routledge
711 Third Avenue, New York, NY 10017

Routledge is an imprint of the Taylor & Francis Group, an informa business

© 2012 Routledge

First edition published by Cavendish Publishing Limited 1997
Seventh edition published by Routledge 2010

British Library Cataloguing in Publication Data
A catalogue record for this book is available from the British Library

ISBN: 978-0-415-68333-3 (pbk)
ISBN: 978-0-203-29294-5 (ebk)

Typeset in Rotis
by RefineCatch Limited, Bungay, Suffolk

MIX
Paper from responsible sources
FSC® C004839
www.fsc.org

Printed and bound in Great Britain by
TJ International Ltd, Padstow, Cornwall

Contents

Table of Cases v

Table of Statutes xiii

How to use this book xix

1 The nature of a crime 1

2 Inchoate offences and participation 25

3 Non-fatal offences against the person 49

4 Fatal offences 69

5 Offences against property 89

6 General defences 113

7 Putting it into practice ... 135

Table of Cases

A (A Juvenile) v R [1978]   102
AG for Northern Ireland v Gallagher [1963]   120
AG's Reference (No 2 of 1991) [1993]   117
AG's Reference (No 1 of 1974) [1974]   110
AG's Reference (No 1 of 1975) [1975]   42
AG's Reference (No 4 of 1979) [1980]   109
AG's Reference (No 6 of 1980) [1981]   58
AG's Reference (No 1 of 1983) [1984]   94
AG's Reference (No 3 of 1992) [1993]   40
AG's Reference (No 3 of 1994) [1997]   22, 23
Attorney General for Jersey v Holley [2005]   77, 78
Atwal v Massey [1971]   112

B v DPP [2000]   21
B and S v Leathley [1979]   99
Blake v DPP [1993]   102, 104
Bratty v AG for Northern Ireland [1963]   117

Cole v Turner [1705]   52
Collins v Wilcock [1984]   52, 58

Doodeward v Spence [1907]   92
DPP v Beard [1920]   120
DPP v Bedder [1954]   76
DPP v Camplin [1978]   72, 78
DPP v Doot [1973]   35
DPP v H [1997]   114
DPP v K and C [1997]   47

DPP v Little [1992]   52
DPP v Majewski [1977]   121
DPP v Morgan [1975]   132, 133, 134
DPP v Newbury and Jones [1976]   83, 84
DPP v Smith [1961]   16
DPP v Smith [2006]   53
DPP v Ray [1974]   108

Fagan v MPC [1968]   10, 52

Gammon v AG of Hong Kong [1985]   21

Hardman and Others v Chief Constable of Avon and   102
    Somerset Constabulary [1986]
Haughton v Smith [1975]   110
Haystead v CC of Derbyshire [2000]   52
Hyam v DPP [1975]   16

JCC v Eisenhower [1984]   55

Lewis v Lethbridge [1987]   94
Logden v DPP [1976]   52
Low v Blease [1975]   92
Luc Thiet Thuan v R [1996]   77

Morphitis v Salmon [1990]   102

National Coal Board v Gamble [1959]   43
Norfolk Constabulary v Seekings and Gould [1986]   99

Oxford v Moss [1979]   92

Re A (Children) (Conjoined twins: surgical   71, 126, 130
    separation) [2001]
R v Abdul-Hussain and Others [1999]   128
R v Adams [1957]   8
R v Adomako [1994]   84

R v Ahluwalia [1992]   77

R v Allen [1985]   108

R v Allen [1988]   120

R v Anderson [1986]   35

R v Anderson and Morris [1966]   45

R v Atkinson [1985]   80

R v B [2006]   60

R v Bailey [1983]   118

R v Bainbridge [1960]   43

R v Barnard [1980]   33

R v Becerra and Cooper [1975]   46

R v Belfon [1976]   57

R v Blaue [1975]   7

R v Bloxham [1983]   111

R v Bowles and Bowles [2004]   39

R v Bourne [1952]   47

R v Brown [1970]   111

R v Brown [1985]   99

R v Brown [1994]   58

R v Burgess [1991]   116

R v Burstow [1997]   52, 55

R v Byrne [1960]   79

R v Caldwell [1982]   18, 103, 121, 124,

R v Calhaem [1985]   43

R v Cambridge [1994]   74

R v Campbell [1991]   37, 38

R v Cato [1976]   9

R v Chan-Fook [1994]   53

R v Cheshire [1991]   8

R v Church [1966]   23, 83

R v Clarkson [1971]   43

R v Cogan and Leak [1975]   47

R v Cole [1994]   128

R v Collins [1972]   99, 100

R v Conway [1989]   127

R v Cunningham [1957]   18

R v Dawson [1976]   97

R v Dawson [1985]	83
R v Dear [1996]	7
R v Dica [2004]	58
R v Dietschmann [2003]	80
R v Dryden [1995]	77
R v Dudley [1989]	103
R v Dudley and Stephens [1884]	126
R v Duffy [1949]	74
R v Dunbar [1957]	79
R v Dytham [1979]	10
R v Doughty [1986]	75
R v Egan [1993]	81
R v English [1997]	44, 46
R v Esop [1836]	131, 134
R v Evans [2009]	84
R v Fernandes [1995]	96
R v Franklin [1883]	83
R v G [2003]	18, 19
R v G [2008]	21
R v Gamble [1989]	45
R v Geddes [1996]	38
R v Gianetto [1997]	43
R v Ghosh [1982]	95
R v Gibbens and Proctor [1918]	10, 13
R v Gilks [1972]	94
R v Gillard [1988]	57
R v Gilmour [2000]	46
R v Gomez [1993]	91
R v Goodfellow [1986]	83
R v Gotts [1991]	128
R v Graham [1982]	128
R v Grainge [1974]	112
R v Griffin [1993]	37
R v Grundy [1977]	46
R v Gullefer [1987]	37
R v Hale [1978]	98
R v Hall [1973]	94

R v Hancock and Shankland [1986]   16, 72
R v Hasan [2005]   128, 132, 134
R v Heard [2007]   122, 124
R v Henderson and Battley [1984]   102
R v Hennessy [1989]   116
R v Hennigan [1971]   6
R v Hinks [2000]   92
R v Horne [1994]   129
R v Howe [1987]   128
R v Hudson and Taylor [1971]   128
R v Humphreys [1995]   75, 77
R v Ibrams [1981]   75
R v Ireland [1997]   52
R v Jackson [1985]   35
R v Jakeman [1983]   23
R v James and Karimi [2006]   77
R v Jordan [1956]   8
R v K [2001]   21
R v Kanwar [1982]   111
R v Kelly [1998]   93
R v Kemp [1957]   116
R v Kennedy [2007]   6, 7, 9, 84
R v Khan [1990]   40
R v Kilneberg and Marsden [1998]   94
R v Kingston [1994]   120
R v Konzani [2005]   58
R v Larsonneur [1933]   14
R v Latimer [1886]   21
R v Le Brun [1992]   23
R v Lidar [2004]   85
R v Lincoln [1980]   112
R v Lipman [1970]   118
R v Lloyd [1985]   96
R v Malcherek and Steel [1981]   71
R v Marcus [1981]   57
R v Marshall, Coombes and Eren [1998]   97
R v Martin [1989]   127

R v Martin [2002]   131
R v Matthews and Alleyne [2003]   15, 16
R v McDavitt [1981]   108
R v Meade and Belt [1823]   52
R v Mellor [1996]   8
R v Michael [1840]   47
R v Miller [1954]   53
R v Miller [1983]   11, 14, 84
R v Mitchell [1998]   46
R v Mohan [1976]   39
R v Moloney [1985]   16
R v Morris [1983]   91
R v Morris [1997]   53
R v Nedrick [1986]   16, 17, 72
R v O'Brien [1974]   33
R v O'Flaherty [2004]   46
R v O'Grady [1987]   133, 134
R v Owino [1995]   130
R v Pagett [1983]   6, 9
R v Pembliton [1874]   21
R v Pitham and Hehl [1976]   91
R v Pitham and Hehl [1977]   112
R v Pittwood [1902]   10, 13
R v Pommell [1995]   127
R v Poulton [1832]   71
R v Powell and Daniels   444
R v Prentice and Others [1993]   84
R v Pritchley [1973]   109
R v Quick [1973]   116, 117
R v Rahman [2008]   45
R v Reeves [1839]   71
R v Richman [1982]   129
R v Roach [2001]   117
R v Roberts [1971]   6, 9, 54
R v Roberts [1987]   112
R v Robinson [1977]   98
R v Rook [1993]   46

R v Rothery [1976] 93
R v Ryan [1995] 100
R v Saunders [1985] 55
R v Savage [1992] 54
R v Scott [1979] 33
R v Shadrokh-Cigari [1988] 94
R v Shaylor [2001] 128
R v Sharpe [1857] 92
R v Shivpuri [1986] 41
R v Siracusa [1989] 36
R v Smith [1959] 8
R v Smith DR [1974] 131, 134
R v Smith and Jones [1976] 100
R v Smith (Morgan) [2001] 77
R v Steer [1980] 103
R v Stewart [2009] 80
R v Stone and Dobinson [1977] 10, 13, 84
R v Sullivan [1984] 55, 116
R v Tabassum [2000] 58
R v Tandy [1989] 80
R v Taylor [2002] 33
R v Thabo Meli [1954] 23
R v Thomas [1985] 52
R v Thornton (No 2) [1996] 75
R v Tolson [1889] 132, 134
R v Tosti [1997] 38
R v Turner No 2 [1971] 93
R v Tyrrell [1894] 47
R v Uddin [1998] 45
R v Vickers [1957] 72
R v Vincent [2001] 108
R v Walker and Hayles [1990] 39
R v Walkington [1979] 99
R v Watson [1989] 83
R v Welsh [1974] 93
R v White [1910] 6, 9
R v Willer [1986] 127

R v Williams (Gladstone) [1984]	130, 133, 134
R v Wilson [1955]	52
R v Wilson [1983]	55
R v Wilson [1996]	59
R v Windle [1952]	116
R v Woodman [1974]	93
R v Woollin [1998]	15, 16, 72
Ricketts v Basildon Magistrates' Court [2010]	93
Roe v Kingerlee [1986]	102
Samuel v Stubbs [1972]	102
Smith v Desmond Hall [1965]	97
Stevens v Gourley [1859]	99
Stewart and Schofield [1995]	46
T v DPP [2003]	53
Thornton v Mitchell [1940]	47
Warner v MPC [1969]	93
Wilcox v Jeffery [1951]	43
Winzar v Chief Constable of Kent [1983]	14
Woolmington v DPP [1935]	2
Yip Chiu-Cheung v R [1994]	36

Table of Statutes

Abortion Act 1967—
  s 1(4)   127
Accessories and Abettors Act 1861—
  s 8   41

Children and Young Persons Act 1933—
  s 50   118
Contempt of Court Act 1981   21
Coroners and Justice Act 2009   71, 73, 74, 77, 78
Corporate Manslaughter and Corporate Homicide Act 2007   85
Crime and Disorder Act 1998   57
  s 29   57
  s 34   118
Criminal Attempts Act 1981   32, 37
  s 1   123
  s 1(1)   37, 110
  s 1(4)   41
  s 1(4)(b)   41
  s 4(3)   37
  s 5   32
Criminal Damage Act 1971   18, 19
  s 1   103
  s 1(1)   4, 5, 100–101, 123
  s 1(2)   101, 123
  s 1(3)   101
  s 5(2)(a)   103
  s 5(2)(b)   127

s 5(3)	104
s 10(1)	101
s 10(2)	101
Criminal Justice Act 1967—	
s 8	16, 17
Criminal Justice Act 1987—	
s 12	36
Criminal Justice Act 1988—	
s 39	53
Criminal Justice and Immigration Act 2008—	
s 76	130
s 76(4)	133, 134
s 76(5)	133, 134
Criminal Law Act 1967—	
s 3(1)	130
s 4(1)	41
s 5(1)	41
Criminal Law Act 1977—	
s 1	123
s 1(1)	32, 36
s 1(1)(b)	34, 36
s 2(1)	34
s 2(2)(a)–(c)	35
s 5(2), (3)	36
Criminal Procedure (Insanity and Unfitness to Plead) Act 1991	115
Fraud Act 2006	104, 105
s 1	104, 105
s 2	105
s 3	105
s 4	105
s 11	107
Homicide Act 1957	78–79
s 2	78
s 2(1)	78, 79

s 3	74, 75
s 4	82
Indecency with Children Act 1960	59
Infant Life (Preservation) Act 1929—	
s 1(1)	127
Infanticide Act 1938—	
s 1(1)	82
Misuse of Drugs Act 1971	121
Offences against the Person Act 1861	53
s 4	28
s 18	15, 51, 53, 55
s 20	39, 51, 53, 55
s 23	18, 51, 57
s 24	51, 57, 123
s 47	51, 53, 54
Perjury Act 1911	
s 4	4
Road Traffic Act 1988—	
s 4	14
Serious Crime Act 2007	
s 44	28–32
s 45	28–32
s 46	28–32
s 47	28–32
s 50	28–32
s 51	28–32
s 65	28–32
s 67	28–32
Sex Offenders Act 1997	59
Sexual Offences Act 1956	21, 59
Sexual Offences Act 1967	59

Sexual Offences Act 2003	20, 21, 39, 51, 59, 65, 68
Pt 2	68
s 1	59, 60, 63, 64, 132
s 1(1)(c)	62
s 1(2)	63
s 2	59, 63, 64
s 3	59, 63, 64, 122
s 4	59, 63, 64, 65
s 63	98
ss 5–8	65
ss 9–15	66, 67
s 74	60, 61, 62
s 75	60, 61, 62
s 76	61, 62
s 78	64
s 79	64
s 79(a)–(c)	64
Theft Act 1968	90
s 1	90, 123
ss 2–6	90
s 2(1)	95
s 2(1)(a)	95
s 2(1)(b)	95
s 2(1)(c)	95
s 2(2)	95
s 3(1)	91
s 4	101
s 4(1)	92
s 4(2)–(3)	92
s 4(2)(a)–(c)	93
s 4(3)	92, 93
s 4(4)	92, 93
s 5(1)	93
s 5(3)	94

s 6(1)	96
s 8	123
s 8(1)	97
s 9	98, 123
s 9(1)(a)	98
s 9(1)(b)	99
s 12	97
s 12A	97
s 21	123
s 22	109, 123
s 22(1)	111
s 25	123
s 34(2)(b)	109
Theft Act 1978–	
s 1(1)	107
s 3	108
s 3(1)	108
s 3(3)	108
Trial of Lunatics Act 1883	
s 2	115

How to use this book

Welcome to this new edition of Routledge Criminal Law Lawcards. In response to student feedback, we've added some new features to these new editions to give you all the support and preparation you need in order to face your law exams with confidence.

Inside this book you will find:

▧ NEW tables of cases and statutes for ease of reference

Table of Cases

Aluminium Industrie Vaasen v Romalpa Aluminium Ltd [1976] 1 WLR 676	14, 15
Andrews v Hopkinson [1956] 3 All ER 422	138
Armour v Thyssen [1990] 3 All ER 481	13
Armstrong v Jackson [1917] 2 KB 822	115
Ashington Piggeries v Hill [1971] 1 All ER 847	53
Barber v NWS Bank [1996] 1 All ER 906	37
Barrow Lane and Ballard v Phillips [1929] 1 KB 574	18, 19
Bartlett v Sidney Marcus [1965] 2 All ER 753	56
Bence Graphics International Ltd v Fasson UK [1998] QB 87	103, 184
Bentinck v Cromwell Engineering [1971] 1 QB 324	172, 173
Bowmakers v Barnett Instruments [1945] KB 65	171, 172
Branwhite v Worcester Works Finance [1969] 1 AC 552	140
Bunge Corporation v Tradax [1981] 2 All ER 513	120
Butterworth v Kingsway Motors [1954] 1 WLR 1286	37
Car and Universal Finance v Caldwell [1965] 1 QB 31	27
Central Newbury Car Auctions v Unity Finance [1957] 1 QB 371	25
Charge Card Services Ltd, Re [1988] 3 All ER 702	92
Clegg v Ole Andersson [2003] 1 All ER 721	66
Clough Mill v Martin [1985] 1 WLR 111	16
Colley v Overseas Exporters [1921] 3 KB 302	121
Couturier v Hastie [1856] 5 HL Cas 673	18
Cundy v Lindsay (1878) 3 App Cas 459	27
Demby Hamilton Ltd v Barden [1949] 1 All ER 435	11
Dimond v Lovell [2000] 2 All ER 897	153
Director General of Fair Trading v First National Bank [2001] 1 All ER 97	83, 185

Table of Statutes

Companies Act 1985	
s 395	14
Companies Act 2006	
s 860	14
Consumer Credit Act 1956	112
Consumer Credit Act 1974	2, 30, 31, 84,
	112, 128, 130,
	144, 145, 147,
	150, 151, 154,
	156, 168
s 8	129, 153
s 9(1)	129
s 11	134
s 12	134
s 15	131
s 17	134
s 19	135
s 33	173
s 34	173
s 39	145
s 39A	145
s 40	145
s 46	147
s 48	145
s 49	147
s 49(1)	145
ss 50–1	147

■ Revision Checklist

We've summarised the key topics you will need to know for your law exams and broken them down into a handy revision checklist. Check them out at the beginning of each chapter, then after you have the chapter down, revisit the checklist and tick each topic off as you gain knowledge and confidence.

Sources of law

1

Primary legislation: Acts of Parliament	■
Secondary legislation	■
Case law	■
System of precedent	■
Common law	■
Equity	■
EU law	■
Human Rights Act 1998	■

■ Key Cases

We've identified the key cases that are most likely to come up in exams. To help you to ensure that you can cite cases with ease, we've included a brief account of the case and judgment for a quick aide-memoire.

HENDY LENNOX v GRAHAME PUTTICK [1984]

Basic facts

Diesel engines were supplied, subject to a *Romalpa* clause, then fitted to generators. Each engine had a serial number. When the buyer became insolvent the seller sought to recover one engine. The Receiver argued that the process of fitting the engine to the generator passed property to the buyer. The court disagreed and allowed the seller to recover the still identifiable engine despite the fact that some hours of work would be required to disconnect it.

Relevance

If the property remains identifiable and is not irredeemably changed by the manufacturing process a *Romalpa* clause may be viable.

■ Companion Website

At the end of each chapter you will be prompted to visit the Routledge Lawcards companion website where you can test your understanding online with specially prepared multiple-choice questions, as well as revise the key terms with our online glossary.

You should now be confident that you would be able to tick all of the boxes on the checklist at the beginning of this chapter. To check your knowledge of Sources of law why not visit the companion website and take the Multiple Choice Question test. Check your understanding of the terms and vocabulary used in this chapter with the flashcard glossary.

▦ Exam Practice

Once you've acquired the basic knowledge, you'll want to put it to the test. The Routledge Questions and Answers provides examples of the kinds of questions that you will face in your exams, together with suggested answer plans and a fully-worked model answer. We've included one example free at the end of this book to help you put your technique and understanding into practice.

QUESTION 1

What are the main sources of law today?

Answer plan

This is, apparently, a very straightforward question, but the temptation is to ignore the European Community (EU) as a source of law and to over-emphasise custom as a source. The following structure does not make these mistakes:

▦ in the contemporary situation, it would not be improper to start with the EU as a source of UK law;

▦ then attention should be moved on to domestic sources of law: statute and common law;

▦ the increased use of delegated legislation should be emphasised;

▦ custom should be referred to, but its extremely limited operation must be emphasised.

ANSWER

European law

Since the UK joined the European Economic Community (EEC), now the EU, it has progressively but effectively passed the power to create laws which are operative in this country to the wider European institutions. The UK is now subject to Community law, not just as a direct consequence of the various treaties of accession passed by the UK Parliament, but increasingly, it is subject to the secondary legislation generated by the various institutions of the EU.

The nature of a crime

Actus reus	
Causation	
Omissions	
Mens rea	
Intention	
Recklessness	
Negligence	
Strict liability	
Transferred malice	

A crime is conduct which has been defined as such by statute or by common law. To be convicted of a crime, two essential elements must be proved:

1 The *Actus Reus* – the prohibited act, omission, or state of affairs; and
2 The *Mens Rea* – the required state of mind, such as intent or recklessness.

The *actus reus* and *mens rea* vary from offence to offence. Every time you deal with a criminal offence you need to break it down into what needs to be proved for the *actus reus* and what needs to be proved for the *mens rea*.

The main exception to this is crimes of strict liability, discussed below.

CRIME = *actus reus* + *mens rea* + absence of a valid defence

The prosecution must prove the existence of the *actus reus* and *mens rea* beyond reasonable doubt. This is sometimes referred to as the *Woolmington* rule (*Woolmington v DPP* [1935]).

GENERAL PRINCIPLES OF CRIMINAL LAW

See diagram on facing page.

CHARACTERISTICS OF AN *ACTUS REUS*

Definition

The *actus reus* consists of all the elements in the statutory or common law definition of the offence except the defendant's mental element. It consists of everything that the prosecution needs to prove except the *mens rea*.

General principles of criminal law

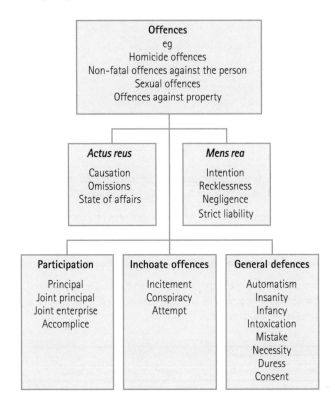

Analysis of the *actus reus*

The *actus reus* can be identified by looking at the definition of the offence in question and subtracting the *mens rea* requirements , which is usually denoted with phrases such as 'knowingly', 'intentionally', 'recklessly', 'maliciously', 'dishonestly' or 'negligently'.

The *actus reus* states the conduct or omission required for the offence, the specified surrounding circumstances in which it must take place and any consequences if required by the offence.

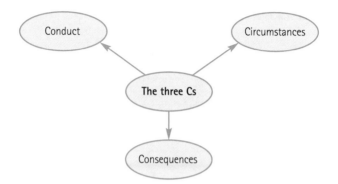

This process of identifying and analysing an *actus reus* can be illustrated in relation to s 1(1) of the Criminal Damage Act 1971, which provides:

> A person who without lawful excuse destroys or damages any property belonging to another intending to destroy or damage any such property or being reckless as to whether such property would be destroyed or damaged shall be guilty of an offence.

Once expressions relating to the *mens rea* requirements of intention or recklessness have been subtracted, the *actus reus* consists of destroying or damaging property belonging to another:

Conduct   = the act of destroying or damaging

Circumstances = the fact that the property must belong to another

Consequences = the resultant damage or destruction

CONDUCT AND RESULT CRIMES

In analysing the *actus reus*, it is possible to distinguish between 'conduct' crimes and 'result' crimes. Conduct crimes punish the actual conduct of the defendant. An example of a conduct crime is perjury. The offence is committed where the defendant makes a statement on oath which he knows to be false or does not believe to be true (s 1 of the Perjury Act 1911). The making of such a statement is sufficient to establish the *actus reus*. The consequence of the statement is irrelevant. It does not matter whether his statement is believed or not.

By contrast, result crimes punish the consequences of the defendant's actions. In a result crime the *actus reus* requires the prosecution to prove that the defendant's conduct caused a particular consequence. An example of a result crime is murder. It must be proved that the defendant caused the victim's death. As we have seen, s1(1) of the Criminal Damage Act 1971 is a result crime. The *actus reus* is that the defendant caused damage to, or destruction of, property belonging to another.

SPECIFIC ISSUES IN ESTABLISHING THE *ACTUS REUS*

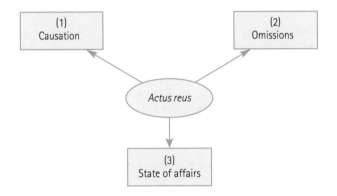

(1) CAUSATION

The question of causation only applies in relation to result crimes. We have seen that result crimes require the prosecution to prove that the defendant's conduct *caused* a particular consequence. Issues of causation do not arise in 'conduct' crimes since they are not concerned with the results and consequences of the defendant's conduct.

Two different forms of causation need to be established:

1 factual causation;
2 legal causation.

Causation is helpfully illustrated in relation to murder. As we will see, part of the *actus reus* of murder is that it must be proved that the defendant caused the victim's death.

Factual causation

The first step in establishing causation is to ask 'was the defendant's act a *cause in fact* of the specified consequence (for example, death in the case of murder)?'. This question can be answered by asking: 'But for what the defendant did would the consequence have occurred?' If the answer is no, causation *in fact* is established.

An example of where the prosecution failed to establish causation in fact is the case of *R v White* [1910]. The defendant had put cyanide into his mother's drink, but the medical evidence showed that she died of heart failure before the poison could take effect. Consequently, the answer to the question 'But for what the defendant did would she have died?' is 'yes'. She would have died anyway.

Legal causation

Just because the prosecution establish that the defendant's act was a cause in fact of the prohibited consequence, does not necessarily mean that the defendant is liable. The prosecution must establish a legal chain of causation between the defendant's acts and the specified consequence. This can become difficult where other individuals or events also contribute to the prohibited harm.

The defendant's act must be a 'substantial' cause of the consequence in question (*R v Cato* [1976]).

It should be noted that 'substantial', in this context, simply means anything more than a *de minimis* (trivial) contribution. For example, in *R v Hennigan* [1971] it was held that the defendant could be found guilty of causing death by dangerous driving even though he was only 20 per cent to blame for the accident.

Also subsequent events must not have broken the chain of causation. An intervening act by the victim will not break the chain of causation unless it is free, deliberate and informed. In *R v Roberts* [1971] the victim jumped from a moving car after the defendant had sexually assaulted her. He claimed that she had broken the chain of causation. The Court disagreed. He was guilty of actual bodily harm (ABH) because her actions were not free, deliberate and informed. Compare this decision with *R v Kennedy* [2007].

An intervening act by a third party will not break the chain of causation unless the act was not a foreseeable consequence of what the defendant had done. In *R v Pagett* [1983], the defendant used his girlfriend as a 'human shield' and fired at the police. The police fired back and killed the girlfriend. The defendant was found guilty of her death. The police fire had not broken the chain of causation because it was foreseeable that the police officers would return fire on the defendant.

> ### ❯ R v KENNEDY [2007]
>
> **The legal chain of causation is broken where the victim is an informed adult of sound mind and their actions are free, deliberate and informed.**
>
> Facts
>
> The defendant supplied the victim with a class A controlled drug. The victim then freely and voluntarily self-administered that drug and died.
>
> Held
>
> The defendant was not liable for the victim's manslaughter. The criminal law generally assumed the existence of free will and, subject to certain exceptions, informed adults of sound mind were treated as autonomous beings able to make their own decision on how to act.

The 'thin skull' rule

As in tort, the defendant must take his victim as he finds him. For example, if the victim of an assault is unusually vulnerable to physical injury as a result of a medical condition or old age, the defendant must accept liability for any unusually serious consequences which result. In *R v Blaue* [1975] it was stated that the defendant had to take 'the whole man, not just the physical man'. The defendant was held to have caused the death of a Jehovah's Witness whom he had stabbed, notwithstanding that she had refused a blood transfusion that would have probably saved her life. He had to take his victim as he found her, including not just her physical condition, but also her religious beliefs.

Self-neglect

Although it may not be reasonably foreseeable that the victim will neglect his wounds, it seems that such neglect will not break the chain of causation. Even if the victim aggravates the condition caused by the defendant, the chain of causation will not be broken. In *R v Dear* [1996] the defendant had repeatedly slashed the victim with a knife after being told that he had sexually interfered with the defendant's 12-year-old daughter. The victim died two days later. The defendant argued that the victim caused his own death by re-opening his wounds and refusing to allow an ambulance to be called, so that he bled to death. There was also evidence of a suicide note left by the victim. The defendant's conviction was nevertheless upheld on the basis that the defendant's conduct was still an operating and significant cause of death.

Death caused by medical treatment

Where death is caused by the medical treatment of a wound, the original attacker is held liable for homicide. This is so even in the case of *negligent* medical treatment (*R v Smith* [1959]).

However, it seems that in rare cases 'palpably wrong' medical treatment will break the chain of causation (*R v Jordan* [1956]). In *R v Cheshire* [1991], it was stated that, unless the negligent treatment was 'so independent of the accused's acts' and 'so potent in causing death' that the contribution made by his acts was insignificant, the chain of causation would not be broken (and see *R v Mellor* [1996]).

There is some authority for the suggestion that the administration of pain-saving drugs which incidentally shorten life by a very short period (hours or days, but not weeks or months) would not amount to a cause in law of death (*R v Adams* [1957]).

▶ R v JORDAN [1956]

Medical treatment will only break the legal chain of causation where the treatment is palpably wrong.

Facts
The victim was stabbed by the defendant and the wound was nearly healed. The victim was then given the wrong medication in hospital from which he died.

Held
The wound was not the operative and substantial cause of death and the medical treatment broke the legal chain of causation. The defendant's conviction for murder was quashed.

Causation

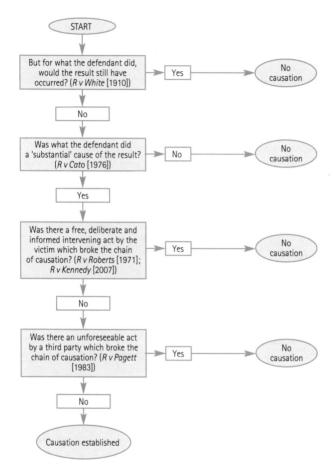

(2) OMISSIONS

As a general rule, a person is not criminally liable for what they do not do. If A sees B drowning and is able to save him by holding out his hand but d abstains from doing, A has committed no offence. There is generally no liability for omissions.

However, there are several exceptions to this rule where the defendant is under a positive duty to act. In these exceptional situations, the defendant will have caused the *actus reus* by doing nothing, a mere omission.

Liability for omissions can occur where there is a duty of care to children or where there is an assumption of care for another. For example, a parent who deliberately neglects a child such that they starve to death may be guilty of murder (*R v Gibbens and Proctor* [1918]). In *R v Stone and Dobinson* [1977] Stone's ill sister came to live with him and his mistress, Dobinson. The sister was initially able to look after herself but her condition deteriorated, and she became bed-ridden. The correct medical help was not sought and she eventually died from extreme neglect. Both defendants were convicted of manslaughter.

Liability may arise where there is a failure to discharge official or contractual obligations. In *R v Pittwood* [1902] a level-crossing operator omitted to close the crossing gates at the appropriate time, causing death to a user. Pittwood was convicted of gross negligence manslaughter. Several statutory provisions also impose criminal sanctions for failure or omission to act. For example, road traffic law makes it an offence to fail to stop after an accident. (See also *R v Dytham* [1979].)

Liability can also arise where there is a failure to avert a danger of one's own making. In *Fagan v MPC* [1968] the defendant parked his car on a police officer's foot by accident but then refused to move the car. While he had committed the *actus reus* of assault by parking the car, he did not have the *mens rea*. Although he did have the *mens rea* when he refused to move that was a mere omission; there was no *actus reus*. He was found guilty on the basis that because although inert he had continued to put pressure on the police officer's foot by keeping the car parked on the police officer's foot. The whole sequence of events constituted a 'continuing act'.

The Continuing Act Theory in *Fagan*

Continuing Act
Actus reus + Mens rea

Fagan parks on policeman's foot, accident.

Potential *actus reus* but no *mens rea*?

Fagan told to move but refuses

Potential *mens rea* present but no *actus reus*? – mere omission?

In *R v Miller* [1983] the defendant was 'sleeping rough' in a building and fell asleep whilst smoking a cigarette. He awoke to find his mattress smouldering but did nothing about the danger – he simply moved to another room and went back to sleep. The fire subsequently spread. He was convicted of arson for his failure to act.

The Court of Appeal in *R v Miller* upheld the conviction using the 'continuing act' theory explained in *Fagan*. The whole of Miller's conduct from the time he lit the cigarette to the time when he moved to another room could be regarded as one act. As such the offence was committed by setting fire to the mattress and failing to put the fire out or to prevent the damage.

However, the House of Lords in *R v Miller* [1983] upheld the conviction but used a different approach. They said that where the defendant accidentally and unwittingly does an act which sets in train a series of events presenting a risk then once the defendant becomes aware of that risk he is under a duty to prevent or reduce the risk. This is known as the 'duty' or 'responsibility' theory.

In *Miller*, Lord Diplock adopted the duty theory rather than the continuing act theory because he felt that it was more easily explained to, and understood by, juries. His lordship preferred to use the term responsibility and not duty because 'duty' suggested an obligation owed in civil rather than criminal law.

Lord Diplock suggested that it was immaterial whether the duty theory or the continuing act theory was applied since both led to the same result. However, it could be said that the duty theory is broader. It could cover the situation where an act is complete but the risk carries on. In contrast, the continuing act requires the act to be on-going. If act is complete, then no continuing act and no liability.

The Responsibility Theory in *Miller*

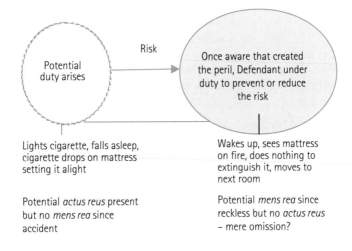

Risk

Potential duty arises

Once aware that created the peril, Defendant under duty to prevent or reduce the risk

Lights cigarette, falls asleep, cigarette drops on mattress setting it alight

Wakes up, sees mattress on fire, does nothing to extinguish it, moves to next room

Potential *actus reus* present but no *mens rea* since accident

Potential *mens rea* since reckless but no *actus reus* – mere omission?

Omissions

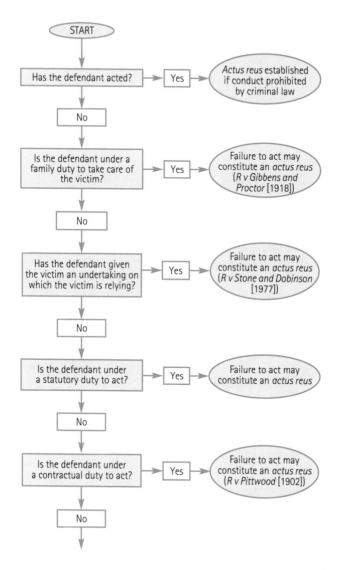

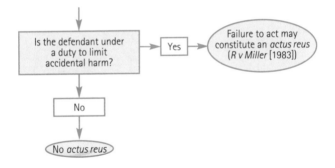

(3) STATE OF AFFAIRS OFFENCES

Exceptionally in some offences the *actus reus* is satisfied if a specific 'state of affairs' is proved to exist. For example, s 4 of the Road Traffic Act 1988 provides that a person who, when in charge of a motor vehicle on a road or other public place, is unfit to drive through drink or drugs, commits an offence. It is not the action of taking charge of the vehicle or that of *becoming* unfit which constitutes the offence, but simply the state of *being unfit.*

Thus, the defendant in *R v Larsonneur* [1933] was convicted of being found in the UK, contrary to the Aliens Order of 1920, despite the fact that she had been forcibly brought into the jurisdiction by the immigration authorities.

Similarly, the defendant in *Winzar v Chief Constable of Kent* [1983] was convicted of being found drunk on the highway, despite the fact that he had been deposited there by police officers.

'State of affairs' offences are often also offences of 'strict liability' (see below). It is not surprising that they tend to be regarded as unjustifiably harsh, since not only is there no need to prove any action by the defendant, but also there is no need to prove any *mens rea* either.

THE NATURE OF *MENS REA*

Definition

The term *mens rea* refers to the mental element in the definition of a crime. This mental element is usually denoted by words such as 'intentionally', 'knowingly', 'recklessly', 'maliciously' or 'negligently', depending on the definition of the crime.

INTENTION

The *mens rea* required for some of the most serious crimes such as murder and wounding or causing grievous bodily harm contrary to s 18 of the Offences against the Person Act 1861 is intention. Intention has an ordinary meaning and a more complex meaning when applied in criminal law. The ordinary meaning is known as 'direct intent'. The defendant intends to do something if that is their purpose. This ordinary definition of intention will be sufficient in most cases.

D ——————▶ Means ——————▶ End (your purpose) = Direct intention

The more complex meaning is often called 'oblique intent' by writers (but not by the courts). This covers the situation where the consequence was not the defendant's purpose but was something that occurred as a result of the defendant's actions. In other words, it covers events which were a side effect of the defendant's actions.

D ——————▶ Means ——————▶ End (your purpose) = Direct intention
             |
     A side effect   Other end   = Oblique intention?

So, if the defendant gave the victim poison with the purpose of killing them then that would be a case of direct intent. There would be no problem in saying that the defendant had the *mens rea* of intention. If, however, the defendant jumped on the victim's back with the purpose of surprising the victim but out of shock that killed them that would possibly be a case of oblique intent.

The courts have struggled with the question of when the jury can infer oblique intent. There are two key questions:

1 Does the defendant need to have foreseen the side effect?
2 How likely is the side effect to occur? Does it have to be virtually certain to occur? Or does it have to be merely probable?

The current law found in *R v Woollin* [1998] and *R v Matthews and Alleyne* [2003] states that the jury cannot infer the side effect unless it was foreseen by the defendant and was virtually certain to occur.

This is a subjective test. Prior to 1967 the test was objective. In *DPP v Smith* [1961] it was held that the side effect is intended if it was a natural and probable consequence of the defendant's acts. This was effectively reversed by s 8 of the Criminal Justice Act 1967 which requires the jury to look at all the evidence to drawing appropriate inference. It provides that the jury are not bound to infer intention if the side effect is a natural and probable consequence; rather the jury should make reference to all the evidence. The courts have interpreted this as requiring a subjective test.

This settled the answer to the first question but led to a series of conflicting decisions concerning the second question. In *Hyam v DPP* [1975] it was held that the *mens rea* was satisfied if the side effect was foreseen as a probable consequence. This effectively eroded the discretion given to the jury under s 8 of the Criminal Justice Act 1967.

In *R v Moloney* [1985] Lord Bridge put forward a 'golden rule': in relation to defining 'intention' is that judges should 'leave it to the jury's good sense to decide'. Lord Bridge held that Judges should generally refrain from giving elaborate directions to the jury on the meaning of intent. It is, after all, a question of fact. However, in rare cases of oblique intent, Lord Bridge said that the jury could infer that the accused inferred a side effect if the side effect was a 'natural consequence' of the defendant's actions and if the defendant foresaw this.

In *R v Hancock and Shankland* [1986] the *Moloney* direction was criticised for not providing a reference to probability.

The Court of Appeal in *R v Nedrick* [1986] provided the following model direction:

> the jury should be directed that they are not entitled to infer the necessary intention unless they feel sure that death or serious bodily harm was a virtual certainty (barring some unforeseen intervention) as a result of the defendant's actions and that the defendant appreciated that such was the case.

In *R v Woollin* [1998] the House of Lords endorsed the *Nedrick* direction but used the word 'find' rather than 'infer'. More recently, in *R v Matthews and Alleyne* [2003] this direction was approved but as a rule of evidence not a rule of law. The Nedrick-Woolin direction preserves the discretion given to the jury under s 8 of the Criminal Justice Act 1967. It states that a jury cannot find intention unless the side effect was virtually certain and the defendant appreciated this; in which case the jury may (rather than must) find intention.

As a result it means that a defendant has intended a result even if it was not their direct intention to do so. This will happen where the jury feel sure that the prohibited harm was virtually certain to happen following the defendant's actions and the jury are also sure that the defendant realised his actions were virtually certain to bring about the harm. This means that different juries may indeed draw different conclusions about the same set of facts.

▶ R v NEDRICK [1986]

Oblique intention cannot be inferred unless the death was virtually certain and the defendant appreciated this.

Facts

The defendant poured paraffin though a letterbox and ignited it with the aim of scarring the woman. The fire killed a child. Did the defendant have the *mens rea* of murder: did he intend to cause death or GBH. The trial judge directed the jury that foresight could be equated with intent.

Held

The defendant's conviction for murder was substituted for manslaughter. The jury should be directed that they are not entitled to infer intention unless they feel sure that death or serious bodily harm was a virtual certainty and that the defendant appreciated this, in which case they may (rather than must) infer that it was intended.

RECKLESSNESS

For many offences, the *mens rea* required is intention or recklessness. Recklessness conveys the notion of taking an unjustified risk. Determining whether something is an unjustified risk is an objective matter. The question that has troubled the courts is whether there should also be a subjective test: is it necessary for the defendant to be aware of the risk before criminal liability can be imposed? Is it necessary for the defendant to be aware of the risk at the time in which he acted or is it sufficient that a reasonably prudent person would have been aware the risk?

D ────────▶ Takes 'unjustified risk' = reckless

Or:

D ────────▶ Foresees + Takes 'unjustified risk' = reckless

The current law found in *R v G* [2003] takes the second approach. A person is reckless if they are aware of the risk and then take the risk. Lord Bingham adopted the definition of 'recklessness' as put forward by the Law Commission:

> A person acts recklessly within the meaning of section 1 of the Criminal Damage Act 1971 with respect to—(i) a circumstance when he is aware of a risk that it exists or will exist; (ii) a result when he is aware of a risk that it will occur; and it is, in the circumstances known to him, unreasonable to take the risk.

This restored the law to the situation that had existed following the earlier decision in *R v Cunningham* [1957]. That case concerned whether the defendant had acted 'maliciously' under s 23 of the Offences against the Person Act 1861. The Court of Appeal adopted Professor Kenny's assertion that 'malice' meant that either intention or recklessness was required and that recklessness required the defendant to have foreseen that the particular kind of harm might be done and to have yet gone on to take the risk.

By contrast, in *R v Caldwell* [1982] the first approach was taken. Lord Diplock said that in addition to covering situations where the defendant is aware of the risk and takes the risk, recklessness also covered the situation where the defendant did an act which created an obvious risk and gave no thought to this or recognised the risk. Lord Diplock said that the *Cunningham* definition of recklessness did not apply to the Criminal Damage Act 1971 since *Cunningham* was concerned with the definition of 'maliciously'.

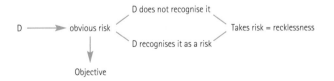

There were two significant problems with the *Caldwell* definition. First, it made those who did not think about the risk as equally culpable as those who did. The reference to an 'obvious' risk meant that defendants would be liable for risks that were obvious to the reasonable person or as Lord Diplock put it, an 'ordinary prudent individual'. Under *Caldwell* children were compared against the standards of the reasonable person. Second, there was a gap in Lord Diplock's judgment. The defendant who stopped, thought and wrongly concluded there was no risk was not reckless. This was known as the '*Caldwell* lacuna' or loophole.

In *R v G* [2003] the House of Lords restored the law to the *Cunningham* definition, adopting a subjective approach. Lord Bingham gave four reasons for doing this. First, the defendant who does not see the risk is not as culpable as the defendant who does see the risk. Stupidity or lack of imagination was not sufficient to expose such a defendant to conviction for a serious crime. Second, it was not moral or just to convict a defendant (least of all a child) on the strength of what someone else would have apprehended if the defendant himself had no such apprehension. Third, the forceful academic, judicial and practitioner criticism of *Caldwell* should not be ignored. Fourth, Lord Diplock in *Caldwell* misinterpreted the Criminal Damage Act 1971 since it was clear from the Law Commission report upon which that Act was based that Parliament did intend to apply the *Cunningham* subjective definition of recklessness.

▶ R v G [2003]

A person is reckless if they are aware of the risk and then take the risk.

Facts

Two boys lit bundles of newspapers and threw them under a wheelie bin when they left. The paper ignited the bins which set alight a nearby building. It was accepted that neither of them appreciated the risk of the fire spreading in the way that it did.

Held

The convictions were quashed: the defendants were not reckless. A person acts recklessly within the meaning of section 1 of the Criminal Damage Act 1971 where he is aware of a risk that exists or will exist and takes the unreasonable risk.

NEGLIGENCE

Some crimes, most notably those under the Sexual Offences Act 2003, require negligence to be proved. As in tort law, negligence is the failure to take reasonable care against a reasonably foreseeable risk.

A defendant is negligent if they fall below the standard of the reasonable person. Negligence is broader than recklessness and covers the *Caldwell* lacuna:

	Is D *Cunningham* Recklessness?	Is D *Caldwell* Recklessness?	Is D negligent?
D sees risk and goes ahead because does not care	Yes	Yes	Yes
D sees risk and goes ahead hoping risk will **not** happen	Yes	Yes	Yes
D sees risk and goes ahead hoping risk will happen	Yes	Yes	Yes
D goes ahead but gives no thought to the risk, which is obvious	No	Yes	Yes
D gives thought to risk (which is obvious) but wrongly concludes that there is no risk and goes ahead	N/A	No	Yes

STRICT LIABILITY

An offence of strict liability is one where the prosecution do not have to prove any *mens rea* in relation to one or more elements of the *actus reus*. At common law, it is thought that there are only three offences of strict liability:

1   Public nuisance (but this is also seen as a tort).
2   Criminal libel (but the tort of libel is more often litigated).
3   Criminal contempt of court (but now see Contempt of Court Act 1981).

In relation to statutory offences, the mere absence of *mens rea* words is not conclusive evidence that Parliament intended the offence to be one of strict liability. Whilst the courts have spoken of 'a presumption' of *mens rea* (*Gammon v AG of Hong Kong* [1985]; *B v DPP* [2000]), the only way to work out whether an offence is one of strict liability is to look at what previous cases have said.

The law on sexual offences against children shows a move towards the increased use of strict liability. In *B v DPP* [2000] and *R v K* [2001] courts had read an implied *mens rea* into offences under the Sexual Offences Act 1956 which were silent as to *mens rea*. This was reversed by the Sexual Offences Act 2003 which created numerous offences of strict liability in relation to child sex offences. The House of Lords in *R v G* [2008] held that this imposition of strict liability is compatible with the European Convention on Human Rights.

Subjective ←				→ Objective
Intention	Subjective recklessness	Objective recklessness	Negligence	Strict liability

TRANSFERRED MALICE

Transferred malice (sometimes called transferred *mens rea*) is a well established, if controversial, principle in criminal law. It is perhaps best explained by reference to the facts of the leading case *R v Latimer* [1886]. D was involved in a quarrel with X in a pub. D removed his belt and swung it towards X but it actually injured V. D was found liable for the unlawful and malicious wounding of V.

The doctrine says that *mens rea* that D has formed 'transfers' over from the *actus reus* that was not completed (wounding X) to the new *actus reus* (wounding V).

The important limitation is that *mens rea* can only be transferred if the same *mens rea* is required for the offence that has been committed. If the defendant intends to kill but the brick he throws actually smashes a window then the *mens rea* cannot be transferred (*R v Pembliton* [1874]).

21

Transferred malice 1

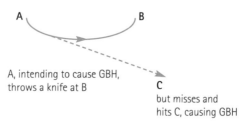

A, intending to cause GBH,
throws a knife at B

C
but misses and
hits C, causing GBH

A is guilty of causing Grievous Bodily Harm (GBH) to C under the doctrine of transferred malice since he has caused the *actus reus* of an offence with the requisite *mens rea* for the same offence.

Transferred malice 2

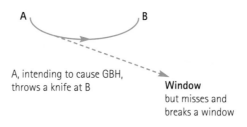

A, intending to cause GBH,
throws a knife at B

Window
but misses and
breaks a window

A is not guilty of criminal damage to the window; the doctrine of transferred malice does not operate since he has caused the *actus reus* of one offence with the *mens rea* of a different offence (however, if the prosecution proved that A was reckless in relation to damaging the window by throwing an object in the vicinity, then he would be liable under normal principles).

In *AG's Reference (No 3 of 1994)* [1997], the House of Lords confirmed the existence of the doctrine of transferred malice, but declined to extend the principle to what it regarded as a 'double transfer' of intent. In this case, the defendant had stabbed a woman whom he knew to be pregnant. She recovered, but there was evidence that the child was born prematurely as a result of the wound to the mother and, as a result of the premature birth, died 120 days later. The House of Lords considered this case to involve a 'double transfer' of intent from the mother to the foetus and from the foetus to the child.

COINCIDENCE OF *ACTUS REUS* AND *MENS REA*

The *mens rea* must coincide at some point in time with the act which causes the *actus reus* (*R v Jakeman* [1983]). However, as we have seen above, the courts are sometimes prepared to hold that the *actus reus* consisted of a continuing act and that the defendant is liable if he formed the requisite *mens rea* at some point during this continuing act.

In *R v Thabo Meli* [1954] the defendants attacked a man in accordance with a preconceived plan. Believing him to be dead, they threw his body over a cliff, making his death look like an accident. Medical evidence revealed that the final cause of his death was in fact exposure at the foot of the cliff. The defendants argued that the act of throwing the victim over the cliff was not accompanied by the requisite *mens rea*. They were nonetheless convicted of murder on the basis that the series of acts resulting in death could not be divided up and it was sufficient that the defendants had the requisite *mens rea* in relation to the first attack.

It seems that the continuing act will continue for as long as the defendant is about the business of committing or covering up the crime (*R v Church* [1966], *R v Le Brun* [1992] and see *AG's Reference (No 3 of 1994)* [1997]).

▶ R v CHURCH [1966]

Although as a general principle the *actus reus* and *mens rea* must coincide, where the *actus reus* occurs after the *mens rea* this may exceptionally be seen as 'one transaction'.

Facts

The defendant hit a prostitute knocking her unconscious. Thinking that she was dead, he threw her body in a river. The victim then drowned.

Held

Although there was no *actus reus* when he hit her and no *mens rea* when she was thrown in the water, the earlier *mens rea* and the later *actus reus* were regarded as one transaction and the defendant was found guilty.

You should now be confident that you would be able to tick all of the boxes on the checklist at the beginning of this chapter. To check your knowledge of The nature of a crime why not visit the companion website and take the Multiple Choice Question test. Check your understanding of the terms and vocabulary used in this chapter with the flashcard glossary.

Inchoate offences and participation

Encouraging or assisting crime

Conspiracy

Attempt

Participation

Joint enterprise

Having looked at the general principles of *actus reus* and *mens rea*, this chapter examines the general principles concerning inchoate offences and participation. Participation is sometimes called complicity, accessory liability or secondary liability.

When we look at particular offences throughout the rest of this book it is important to remember that the criminal law is not just concerned with substantive liability. Defendants may be charged with preparing to complete a criminal offence (inchoate liability) or with helping another to commit an offence (secondary liability).

The law in this area has been subject to recent reform. The new inchoate offence of encouraging or assisting crime has replaced the common law offence of incitement. This has also affected the law on participation. The Law Commission has advocated further reform of the law on attempt but no statutory changes have yet been made.

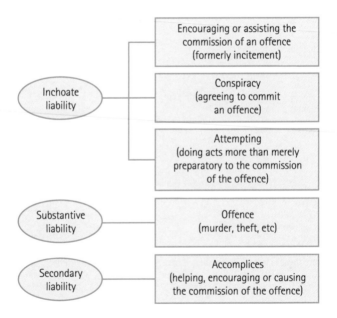

INCHOATE LIABILITY

Inchoate liability can occur where the defendant progresses some way towards the commission of an offence, but does not necessarily commit the completed offence.

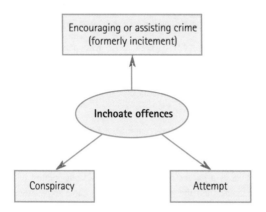

There is no liability for criminal thoughts or for simply telling your thoughts to another. However, once some step is taken, the defendant may be liable for an inchoate offence.

Inchoate offences permit intervention at an earlier stage before any harm has been done but at a time when the accused has moved from mere mental planning to the stage of performing overt acts which manifest his intention that a substantive offence be committed.

There are three inchoate crimes: assisting or encouraging crime (which was formerly known as incitement), conspiracy and attempt.

Those convicted of inchoate offences are liable to the same penalty as if they had been convicted of the relevant substantive offence. A defendant may be charged with an inchoate offence either where the substantive offence is not completed or where there is insufficient evidence to prove the substantive offence.

The inchoate offence must be linked to a substantive offence. A defendant cannot be charged with 'attempt' but can be charged with 'attempted murder'.

ENCOURAGING OR ASSISTING CRIME

Part 2 of the Serious Crime Act 2007 has abolished the common law on incitement, replacing the common law inchoate offence of incitement with three new inchoate offences of encouraging or assisting crime. In addition, Parliament has created certain statutory offences of incitement, such as incitement to murder contrary to s 4 Offences Against the Person Act 1861. These are unaffected by the 2007 Act and are governed by similar principles as incitement at common law.

At common law, incitement covered those who persuaded or encouraged another to do an act or acts, intending to bring about a crime. The defendant could be charged regardless of whether the crime was ever committed. If the crime was committed they would have been an accessory (see 'Participation' below).

The defect in the common law was that incitement did not cover assisting crime. If a defendant encouraged or assisted someone to commit an offence and the person committed or attempted to commit the offence then the defendant would be liable as an accessory. If the person did not commit or attempt to commit the crime then the defendant could be liable for incitement if they encouraged the offence; if they only assisted an offence that the defendant did not commit or attempt to commit then the defendant incurred no criminal liability.

Action by the defendant	Potential liability before October 2008
Encourages crime which is committed	Secondary liability – Accessory
Encourages crime which is not committed	Inchoate liability – Incitement
Assists crime which is committed	Secondary liability – Accessory
Assists crime which is not committed	No liability

Part 2 of the Serious Crime Act 2007 seeks to redress this defect. Sections 45 to 46 of the Act create three new inchoate offences.

Section 44
Section 44 covers those who encourage or assist intending a criminal end.

The *actus reus* is doing an act which is capable of encouraging or assisting another to commit a criminal offence.

The *mens rea* is intending to encourage or assist the other to commit an offence. This requires direct intent. Oblique intent will not suffice: the defendant is 'not to be taken to have intended to encourage or assist the commission of an offence merely because such encouragement or assistance was a foreseeable consequence of his act' (s 44(2)).

Section 45

Section 45 covers those who encourage or assist believing that there is a criminal end that that their act will help but not intending it.

The *actus reus* is the same as for s 44: doing an act which is capable of encouraging or assisting another to commit a criminal offence.

The *mens rea* is believing that the offence will be committed and that the act will encourage or assist its completion.

Section 46

Section 46 covers those who encourage or assist believing that one or more offences will be committed without believing which one, but generally believing that their act will help.

The *actus reus* is doing an act which is capable of encouraging or assisting another to commit one or more of a number of criminal offences.

The *mens rea* is believing that one or more of those offences will be committed (without any belief as to a particular crime) and that this act will encourage or assist the completion of one or more of those offences.

Further provisions

The rest of Part 2 provides further details in relation to all three inchoate offences. In relation to the *actus reus*, 'encouraging' includes threatening or putting pressure on another person to commit an offence (s 65(1)). 'Act' includes a course of conduct (s 67) and 'doing of an act' includes a failure to act, the continuation of an act that has already begun and an attempt to do an act (s 47(8)).

An act which is 'capable of encouraging or assisting another to commit a criminal offence' includes 'taking steps to reduce the possibility of criminal proceedings being brought' or 'failing to take reasonable steps to discharge a duty' (s 65(2)).

In relation to the *mens rea*, s 47(5) is of importance. It states that where the offence that the defendant is assisting or encouraging requires *mens rea* then it must be proved that either (i) the defendant believed that the defendant would have the *mens rea* required, (ii) the defendant was reckless as to whether or not the defendant would have the *mens rea* required or (iii) if the defendant's state of mind was such that he would have *mens rea* required if he were to do the act.

It also states that where the offence that the defendant is assisting or encouraging requires proof of particular circumstances or consequences then it must be proved that either (i) the defendant believed that the act would be done in those circumstances or with those consequences or (ii) the defendant was reckless as to whether or not the act would be done in those circumstances or with those consequences.

Defences

There also exists a defence of acting reasonably under s 50. For example, a motorist who changes motorway lanes to allow a speeding motorist to overtake them assists that offence. However, their actions are likely to be considered reasonable under s 50.

Under s 51 where an offence exists to protect a particular category of persons a person who falls within that category cannot be charged with encouraging or assisting a crime where that crime is against them. For example, an underage girl who encourages a man to have illegal sex with her cannot be charged with encouraging or assisting that offence. This gives effect to the rule in *R v Tyrell* [1894].

Impossibility

At common law, a defendant could not be guilty of an inchoate offence if the substantive crime was impossible to commit. This only applied where the criminal end itself was impossible. A could not be liable for inciting B to kill C if C was already dead. This defence did not apply where the crime was only impossible because of the means. A could be liable for inciting B to shoot C even if the gun given to C turned out to be defective.

This common law defence has been removed in the statutory inchoate offences of conspiracy and attempt. There is some doubt as to whether impossibility is a

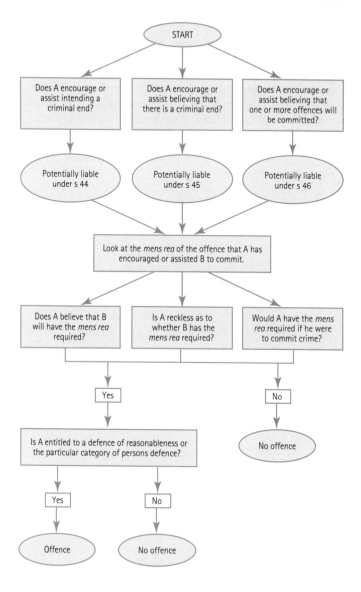

defence to the new statutory inchoate offences of encouraging or assisting crime. Generally the focus of the new law is on the person doing the encouraging or assisting and what they believed as opposed to the effect of that encouraging or assisting. However, ss 44 to 46 provide that an act must be capable of encouraging or assisting another to commit a criminal offence in order for there to be liability. This would seem to indicate that a defendant who does an act which is incapable of encouraging or assisting a crime is not liable.

CONSPIRACY

Section 1(1) of the Criminal Law Act 1977 created a statutory offence of conspiracy and abolished, with two exceptions, the old common law offence of conspiracy.

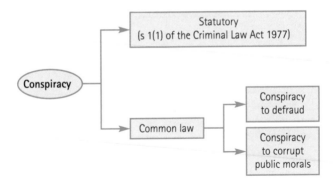

STATUTORY CONSPIRACY

Definition

The statutory offence of conspiracy is created by s 1(1) of the Criminal Law Act 1977, as amended by s 5 of the Criminal Attempts Act 1981, which provides:

... if a person agrees with any other person or persons that a course of conduct shall be pursued which, if the agreement is carried out in accordance with their intentions, either:

(a) will necessarily amount to or involve the commission of any offence or offences by one or more of the parties to the agreement; or

(b) would do so but for the existence of facts which render the commission of the offence or any of the offences impossible,

he is guilty of conspiracy to commit the offence or offences in question.

Actus reus

The *actus reus* of a statutory conspiracy consists of an agreement between two or more persons to embark on a 'course of conduct' that will necessarily involve the commission of an offence by one of the parties.

It appears that merely talking about the possibility of committing an offence is not sufficient to constitute an agreement (*R v O'Brien* [1974]).

The parties must agree to commit the same crime. In *R v Taylor* [2002] where the first defendant agreed to import Class A drugs and the second defendant agreed to import Class B drugs no conspiracy had occurred.

Where the parties have agreed to commit the same crime, the conspiracy to commit that crime is complete as soon as the agreement has been made. Liability remains regardless of whether the agreed offence is committed or if a party changes their mind (*R v Barnard* [1980]).

The agreement must be communicated between the parties to the conspiracy (*R v Scott* [1979]).

However, it is not necessary for every party to a conspiracy to be aware of the existence of every other party. The agreement can take the form of a *chain*, where A agrees with B who then agrees with C and so on, a *wheel*, where numerous parties agree on the same course of conduct with one central figure, or a *cluster*, where several parties simultaneously agree.

Chain

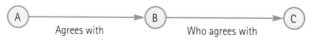

A —— Agrees with —→ B —— Who agrees with —→ C

Wheel

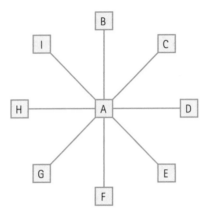

Cluster

A person cannot be guilty of conspiracy to commit an offence if he is an intended victim of that offence (s 2(1) of the Criminal Law Act 1977).

Section 1(1), para (b) of the Criminal Law Act 1977 makes it clear that, as far as *statutory* conspiracy is concerned, the fact that the agreement is impossible to carry out is no bar to liability (impossibility may still be a defence to a charge of common law conspiracy).

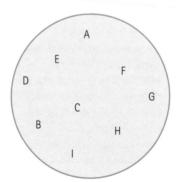

A person shall not be guilty of conspiracy if the only other person with whom he agrees is his spouse (s 2(2)(a)); a child under the age of 10 (s 2(2)(b)); or an intended victim of the agreed offence (s 2(2)(c)).

If the words 'necessarily amount to ... the commission of any offence' were construed strictly, it would be impossible to secure any convictions for conspiracies to commit *possible* offences. For example, suppose that A agrees with B to put a deadly poison into C's food. At first sight, this appears to be a clear case of conspiracy to murder, but it could be argued that this course of conduct would not *necessarily* have amounted to the offence in question; C might not be hungry, or might drop the plate, or might not die. Paradoxically, if the offence was impossible, perhaps because C was already dead at the time of the agreement, then there would be liability for conspiracy to murder since, as we have seen, impossibility is no defence.

In order to avoid this kind of anomalous result, the courts have interpreted 'necessarily' not to mean that the offence must inevitably be committed but that the offence would be necessarily committed *if* the agreement was carried out in accordance with the conspirators' intentions (*R v Jackson* [1985]). According to this interpretation, A and B would be guilty of conspiracy to murder since the intended result of their common plan was the death of C.

Liability arises at the time agreement is reached and continues until it is carried out or abandoned: *DPP v Doot* [1973].

Mens rea

There appear to be two elements to the *mens rea* for conspiracy. First, each defendant should have knowledge of any facts or circumstances specified in the substantive offence. Secondly, each defendant should intend the conspiracy to be carried out and the relevant offence committed.

Difficulties have arisen with the second element. In *R v Anderson* [1986] a co-conspirator (the defendant) provided wire cutters to another prisoner to facilitate an escape; the defendant claimed that his only interest was money and that he did not believe the escape would succeed and therefore could not have intended it. In upholding a conviction for conspiracy, Lord Bridge decided, firstly, that a defendant can be convicted of conspiracy without having the intention that the agreement be carried out, and secondly, it is sufficient *mens*

35

rea if, and only if, the defendant intended to play some part in the agreed course of conduct in furtherance of the criminal purpose.

Both propositions are now widely considered to be wrong but they have not been expressly overruled. The first proposition is difficult to reconcile with s 1(1) of the Criminal Law Act 1977 which requires there to be an agreement which if carried out *in accordance with their intentions* would necessarily amount to the commission of an offence. The Privy Council subsequently held in *Yip Chiu-Cheung v R* [1994] that it must be established that each conspirator intended the agreement to be carried out, but *R v Anderson* remains the higher authority.

Lord Bridge's second proposition has also been criticised, as it would appear to exclude from the criminal sanction those who plan but do not take part in offences ('godfathers'). This proposition was 'radically' re-interpreted by the Court of Appeal in *R v Siracusa* [1989], such that agreeing 'to play some part' would include doing nothing to stop the unlawful activity.

Note that it was accepted in *R v Siracusa* that the *mens rea* sufficient to support the substantive offence will not necessarily suffice for conspiracy to commit that offence. For example, while the lesser intention to do grievous bodily harm is sufficient *mens rea* to commit murder, the *full* intention to kill is required to support a charge of conspiracy to murder. See below in relation to the *mens rea* for an attempt.

COMMON LAW CONSPIRACY
Section 5(2) and (3) of the Criminal Law Act 1977 preserves two forms of common law conspiracy: conspiracy to defraud and conspiracy to corrupt public morals or outrage public decency.

Common law or statutory conspiracy?
According to s 12 of the Criminal Justice Act 1987, statutory conspiracy and common law conspiracy are not mutually exclusive. The prosecution can choose which offence to charge in cases of overlap.

Impossibility
Impossibility is no defence to a charge of statutory conspiracy (s 1(1)(b) of the Criminal Law Act 1977), but may be a defence to a common law conspiracy.

ATTEMPT

By s 1(1) of the Criminal Attempts Act 1981:

> If with intent to commit an offence to which this section applies, a person does an act which is more than merely preparatory to the commission of the offence, he is guilty of attempting to commit the offence.

The judge decides whether there is sufficient evidence to put to the jury, but it is the jury who must decide whether the defendant's acts have gone beyond mere preparation and thus come within the s 1(1) definition of an attempt (*R v Griffin* [1993] and see s 4(3) of the Criminal Attempts Act 1981).

Actus reus

The *actus reus* is doing an act which is more than merely preparatory to the commission of the offence.

It must be proved that the defendant has gone beyond mere preparation, although it is no longer necessary for the 'last act' prior to the commission of the offence to have been committed (*R v Gullefer* [1987]).

Lord Lane in *Gullefer* said that the 1981 Act sought to steer a 'midway course' between mere preparation, on the one hand, and the 'last act' necessary to commit the offence on the other. He went on to state that the attempt begins 'when the defendant embarks on the crime proper'.

▶ R v CAMPBELL [1991]

To be liable of a criminal attempt the defendant must have done an act that is more than merely preparatory.

Facts

The defendant was arrested close to the post office where he intended to commit a robbery equipped with an imitation firearm that was not drawn.

Held

These acts did not equate to acts that were more than merely preparatory.

Mere preparation	Liability for attempt 'midway course'	The 'last act'
for example, buying the gun	taking aim	pulling the trigger

It seems that the courts take a relatively restricted view of what amounts to going beyond mere preparation. For example, in *R v Campbell* [1991], the defendant, who was armed with (but had not drawn) an imitation firearm, was arrested within a yard of the door of a post office which he intended to rob. Nevertheless, the Court of Appeal held that there was no evidence on which a jury could 'properly and safely' find that the defendant's acts were more than merely preparatory. Similarly, in *R v Geddes* [1996], another borderline case, the defendant was found in the boys' toilet of a school, equipped with lengths of string, sealing tape and a knife. He was charged and convicted of attempted false imprisonment, but successfully appealed. Although there was no doubt about the defendant's intention, it was held that the evidence showed no more than that he had made preparations, got himself ready and positioned himself ready to commit the offence. He had not had any contact with any potential victim, nor could it be said that he had moved from the role of preparation and planning into the area of execution or implementation. In short, there was no evidence that he did anything more than merely preparatory actions.

In *R v Tosti* [1997], the two accused had provided themselves with oxyacetylene equipment, driven to the scene of a planned burglary, concealed the equipment in a hedge, approached the door of a barn and examined the padlock on it. They then became aware that they were being watched and ran off. They were convicted of attempted burglary and their subsequent appeal was dismissed.

The distinction between *R v Geddes* and *R v Tosti* is that, in the former case, the evidence did not show that the defendant had made contact with a victim (that is, a child to imprison), whereas, in the latter, the accused had made contact with a target (that is, the barn to burgle). Presumably, it was when the accused started to 'examine' the padlock that they moved beyond planning and preparation to execution.

In *R v Bowles and Bowles* [2004] the defendants prepared a will, favouring themselves, for an elderly neighbour. They did not however execute it but left it in a drawer. Their conduct was deemed to be merely preparatory towards making a false instrument.

Mens rea

The general principle is that the defendant must have the *full* intention to commit the offence in question (*R v Mohan* [1976]). For example, on a charge of attempted murder, intending to do GBH would not suffice; there must be an intention to kill. However, an indirect intention (foresight of consequence as a virtual certainty) was held to be sufficient in *R v Walker and Hayles* [1990]. In that case the defendants had threatened to kill the victim and dropped him from a third floor balcony. The convictions for attempted murder were upheld.

It was assumed that the intention was required as to every element of the *actus reus*. This means that the *mens rea* for an attempt can be greater than the *mens rea* for the substantive offence. This compensates for the weaker than usual *actus reus*.

For example, whilst a defendant can be convicted under s 20 of the Offences against the Person Act 1861 of recklessly causing a wound, a charge of attempting to wound requires intention to wound. **The defendant needs to have intended the consequence.**

Some crimes, however, require *mens rea* in relation to a circumstance rather than a consequence. For example, in relation to rape, the *actus reus* is both conduct (penetration) and circumstance (lack of consent). The *mens rea* for the substantive offence is satisfied if the defendant intended to penetrate and was negligent as to whether the victim (V) consented.

Rape:

Actus reus:	(1) Penetration	(2) V does not consent
Mens rea:	(1) Intention to penetrate	(2) Negligent as to whether V consents

(Note that previously, the defendant needed to be reckless (rather than negligent) about whether V consented. The Sexual Offences Act 2003 changed this but many of the cases on attempted rape concern the old law.)

To charge a defendant with attempted rape do you need to prove that they intended both aspects of the *actus reus*, the conduct and the circumstances?

The Court of Appeal has decided that where the *actus reus* element is a circumstance. If recklessness (or a lower fault element) as to circumstances suffices for the substantive offence, then recklessness (or a lower fault element) as to circumstances will suffice for the attempt (*R v Khan* [1990]).

So, to be able to charge the defendant with attempted rape, you need to prove the defendant intended to penetrate and was negligent as to whether the victim consents.

Attempted Rape:

Actus reus:	(3) An act which is more than merely preparatory	
Mens rea:	(1) Intention to penetrate	(2) Negligent as to whether V consents

The Court of Appeal in *AG's Reference (No 3 of 1992)* [1993] proposed an alternative test: the 'missing element' approach. This states that the defendant only needs to intend the missing element that prevented the offence from being a successful crime. In relation to all other elements, it is sufficient that the defendant had the *mens rea* required for the substantive offence.

For example, in relation to rape, the defendant may be charged with attempted rape because although he sought to have penetration with a woman who does not consent, there was no penetration. The missing element is thus penetration. So according to *AG's Reference (No 3 of 1992)*, it is necessary to prove that the defendant intended to have penetration but not necessary to prove that he intended to have penetration without consent. The normal fault element (negligence) would apply in relation to consent.

Impossibility

It is now clear that impossibility will be no defence to a charge of attempt. Section 1(2) of the Criminal Attempts Act 1981 states:

> A person may be guilty of attempting to commit an offence to which this section applies even thought the facts are such that the commission of the offence is impossible.

In *R v Shivpuri* [1986] the defendant was found in possession of a suitcase containing bags of a white substance. He confessed to receiving and distributing what he assumed to be an illegally imported drug. The substance turned out not to be a prohibited drug but he was still guilty of an attempt to commit the relevant offences of dealing with and harbouring A and B class drugs.

Does impossibility negate liability?	
Incitement	Yes
Conspiracy	No
Attempt	No

Offences that can be attempted

Generally, any offence triable in England and Wales as an indictable offence (that is, any offence triable only on indictment, or triable either way) may be attempted (s 1(4) of the Criminal Attempts Act 1981).

However, the following offences cannot be attempted:

- statutory or common law conspiracy;

- offences of assisting an arrestable offender or compounding an arrestable offence contrary to s 4(1) and s 5(1) of the Criminal Law Act 1967;

- aiding, abetting, counselling or procuring the commission of an offence (s 1(4)(b) of the Criminal Attempts Act 1981).

PARTICIPATION

A defendant can be liable as a principal or as an accessory to an offence.

- *Principal*: the actual perpetrator of the offence.

- *Accessory*: one who aids, abets, counsels or procures the commission of the offence. Generally, liability as an accessory can arise in relation to any offence.

Section 8 of the Accessories and Abettors Act 1861 provides:

> Whosoever shall aid, abet, counsel, or procure the commission of [any offence], shall be liable to be tried, indicted, and punished as a principal offender.

Therefore the distinction between an accessory and a principal offender is of little importance in many cases.

Definition of accessorial liability: *actus reus*

In practice, the phrase 'aid, abet, counsel or procure' is commonly used as a whole without defining which of the four constituent words correctly encapsulates the defendant's conduct. However certain authorities have attempted to isolate the precise meanings of the words. Generally, 'aid' and 'abet' are considered to cover assistance and encouragement given at the time of the offence, whereas 'counsel' and 'procure' more often describe advice and assistance given at an earlier stage. The four modes of accessorial participation have also been differentiated in terms of requirements of causation and consensus (see table below).

Action	Time	Causation required?	Consensus required?
Aiding, that is, helping	Before or during offence	Yes (1)	No
Abetting, that is, encouraging	During offence	No	Yes
Counselling, that is, encouraging or threatening	Before offence	Yes (2)	Yes
Procuring, that is, causing	Before offence	Yes (3)	No

(1) Causation is required in the sense that the defendant must assist the principal to commit the offence earlier, more easily or more safely.
(2) Counselling must have had some effect on the principal's mind.
(3) Direct causation required.

▪ Procuring: there must be a causal link to the principal's act, but there is no requirement of consensus. For example, if a defendant secretly laces another person's drink, and that person is then subsequently convicted of drink driving, the defendant will be liable for procuring the offence in having brought it about, despite there being no meeting of minds (*AG's Reference (No 1 of 1975)*).

▪ Counselling: requires less of a causal link. A person can counsel a principal who has already decided to commit the crime (*R v Gianetto* [1997]). It need only be shown that the counsellor had some effect on the principal's mind. However, there does need to be some meeting of minds in so far as the act done must be within the scope of the authority or advice given by the counsellor (*R v Calhaem* [1985]).

Mens rea

The requisite *mens rea* consists of (1) an *intention* to aid, abet, etc, and (2) knowledge of the crime the principal intends to commit.

Intention to aid does not require the defendant's purpose or motive to be that the principal offence should be committed. For example, Devlin J said in *National Coal Board v Gamble* [1959]:

> If one man deliberately sells to another a gun to be used for murdering a third, he may be indifferent about whether the third man lives or dies and interested only in the cash profit to be made out of the sale, but he can still be an aider and abettor. To hold otherwise would be to negative the rule that *mens rea* is a matter of intent only and does not depend on desire or motive.

Difficulties may arise in relation to *knowledge* where the offence is to be committed in the future or by a person of whose precise intentions the accused cannot be certain. An example is where the defendant knows that a burglary is to be committed and provides equipment to be used in the burglary. He is guilty even if he does not know of the precise details of the proposed offence, provided that he knows the *type of crime* to be committed (*R v Bainbridge* [1960]).

Mere presence at the scene

There will be no intention to aid (or encourage) where the defendant was merely present at the scene of the crime and he did not personally appreciate the natural and probable consequences of his action. For example, in *R v Clarkson* [1971] two drunken soldiers entered a room to find other soldiers raping a woman and remained on the scene to watch. They were found not to have an intention to encourage. Obviously abetting or counselling will occur where a spectator applauds or purchases a ticket for an illegal performance (*Wilcox v Jeffery* [1951]).

Liability in cases of joint enterprise

Where individuals act together in the execution of a crime, it is clear that defendants may be charged as joint principals, for example where two individuals undertake an attack and one holds and the other stabs the victim. However, difficulties have arisen in defining liability where individuals co-participate in a crime but in the course of committing the crime one of them goes beyond the scope of action intended by the others. In response, the courts have developed a doctrine of joint enterprise, particularly in relation to the offence of homicide.

This doctrine of joint enterprise has developed through a line of authorities and appears to have culminated in the twin-case decision of the House of Lords in *R v Powell and Daniels*; *R v English* [1997]. The doctrine states that an accomplice to a principal who kills can be guilty of murder if he foresees that the principal *might* kill or do grievous bodily harm (GBH) – he does not himself have to have the intention to kill or do GBH. Furthermore, the accomplice might not be present at the actual killing – he may be sitting in the getaway car or be in another part of the house; he may have hoped, and probably did hope, that the principal would not kill or do serious injury, however if the accomplice foresees the possibility that the principal might kill or do GBH as part of their joint enterprise, then he is liable to be convicted of murder. Therefore, an accomplice can be convicted of murder with a lesser degree of *mens rea* than the actual killer, who must have the *mens rea* himself to kill or do GBH.

▶ R v ENGLISH [1997]

An accomplice to a principal who kills can be guilty of murder if he foresees that the principal might kill or do grievous bodily harm (GBH) – he does not have to have the intention to kill or do GBH.

Facts

The defendant agreed to assault a police officer with wooden posts. During the attack the principal stabbed the officer to death. The defendant had no knowledge that the principal had brought a knife to the attack.

> **Held**
>
> Where the principal acts in a fundamentally different way to that foreseen by the defendant, the defendant will not be liable for murder as a secondary party.

However, even in cases where the accomplice foresees death or GBH, he may escape liability for murder where the principal offender causes death by an act fundamentally different from that foreseen:

Scenario 1

The accomplice does not contemplate the use of the weapon and the principal kills with a weapon (*R v Anderson and Morris* [1966]). However, if the principal produces a weapon and the accomplice continues to participate in the crime he will be liable (*R v Uddin* [1998]).

Scenario 2

The accomplice foresees the use of a non-deadly weapon (eg a baseball bat) and the principal elects to use a deadly weapon (eg a gun). In *R v Gamble* [1989] the accomplice escaped liability where he foresaw the use of a gun to 'kneecap' but the principal offenders proceeded to kill the victim. By contrast, if the weapon used is different from, but as dangerous as, that contemplated by the accomplice, he will not escape liability: for example if he contemplated the use of a knife and the principal uses a gun to kill.

In *R v Rahman* [2008] the House of Lords has confirmed that the accessory is not liable where the principal suddenly produces and uses a weapon of which the accessory knows nothing and which is more lethal than any weapon contemplated, for that reason the principal's act is to be regarded as fundamentally different from anything foreseen. This 'fundamental difference' test was followed in *R v Yemoh* [2009].

A point that remains unresolved in this area of law is whether, having escaped liability for murder, the accomplice should be liable for manslaughter (see Chapter 4). In the major line of cases the answer appears to be no. In *R v Anderson and Morris* the accomplice foresaw an attack on the victim but not serious harm; he was unaware that the principal had a knife. The principal stabbed the victim to death. The court held that the accomplice should not be convicted of manslaughter since the principal completely departed from the

45

common design. A similar approach was adopted in *R v English* [1997]. However, a conviction for manslaughter was upheld in *R v Stewart and Schofield* [1995] and in *R v Gilmour* [2000]. In *Gilmour* the accomplice drove the car for two principals who petrol bombed a house, killing three child occupants. The accomplice knew that the house was to be petrol bombed but had not foreseen that serious harm would ensue. By contrast, the principals had intent to do GBH. The Court of Appeal held that the accomplice could be found guilty of manslaughter on the basis that the principals carried out the very deed (*actus reus*) contemplated by the accomplice.

The fact that the accomplice had not foreseen serious harm meant that he could not be liable for murder, but nonetheless he had sufficient *mens rea* to be convicted of manslaughter. Cases such as *Anderson* and *English* were distinguished in that the principal offenders in those cases departed from the *actus reus* contemplated by the accomplice, whereas in *Stewart* and *Gilmour* the principals carry out the very act contemplated, albeit with greater *mens rea* than the accomplice.

Withdrawal from the common plan

What will amount to an effective withdrawal will depend upon which mode of participation the accomplice has engaged in. If the defendant has assisted or encouraged the commission of the offence prior to its commission, then it seems that all that is required is that the defendant clearly communicates his withdrawal from the common plan (*R v Grundy* [1977]; *R v Rook* [1993]).

Where the defendant aids or abets at the scene of the crime, then much more will be required in order to constitute an effective withdrawal. Indeed, in these circumstances, nothing less than physical intervention may be required (*R v Becerra and Cooper* [1975]). However, in the case of spontaneous, as opposed to pre-planned, violence, a participant can effectively withdraw from the joint enterprise without necessarily communicating that withdrawal to the other parties (*R v Mitchell* [1998]).

Where there is an issue as to whether there have been one or two incidents leading onto a fatal attack, the jury have to be satisfied that the fatal injuries were sustained when the joint enterprise was continuing and that a particular defendant was still acting within that joint enterprise (*R v O'Flaherty* [2004]).

Victims as accomplices

In *R v Tyrrell* [1894], a girl below the age of 16 was found not guilty of aiding and abetting a man to have unlawful sexual intercourse with her. The principle was that a victim cannot incur liability as an accomplice if the offence in question is one that was designed to protect a class of people of which the victim is a member.

Acquittal of the principal

If the principal is acquitted because he has not committed the *actus reus* of the offence in question, then the defendant will not be liable as an accomplice as there is no offence of assisting or encouraging (*Thornton v Mitchell* [1940]). However, even if the principal has not committed the *actus reus* of the full offence, he may still be liable for attempt. In these circumstances, the defendant could be liable for aiding and abetting the attempt.

If the principal is acquitted because he can avail himself of some defence which is not available to the defendant, there is nothing to prevent the conviction of the defendant as an accomplice (*R v Bourne* [1952]).

If the principal is acquitted because he lacks the *mens rea* or capacity for the crime in question, the defendant may still incur liability either as a principal who has acted through an innocent agent (*R v Michael* [1840]) or as an accomplice (*R v Cogan and Leak* [1975]; *DPP v K and C* [1997]).

	Accomplice liable?	
	Yes	No
Principal lacks *actus reus*		✓
Principal lacks *mens rea*	✓	
Principal lacks capacity	✓	
Principal has defence not available to accomplice	✓	
Accomplice is a victim		✓

The Law Commission (2007) published a report urging reform of the law on participation at the same time as its report on encouraging or assisting crime. Although the proposals on encouraging or assisting crime have been enacted in

Part 2 of the Serious Crime Act 2007, the proposals on participation have not. The new inchoate offences of encouraging or assisting crime now overlap with the unreformed law on participation.

You should now be confident that you would be able to tick all of the boxes on the checklist at the beginning of this chapter. To check your knowledge of Inchoate offences and participation why not visit the companion website and take the Multiple Choice Question test. Check your understanding of the terms and vocabulary used in this chapter with the flashcard glossary.

Non-fatal offences against the person

Assault and battery	
s 47 OAPA 1861	
s 20 OAPA 1861	
s 18 OAPA 1861	
ss 23, 24 OAPA 1861	
Consent	
Rape	
Assault by penetration	
Sexual assault	
Causing a person to engage in a sexual activity without consent	

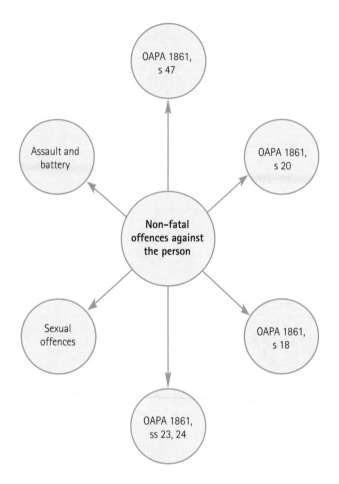

Having looked at the general principles of *actus reus*, *mens rea*, inchoate offences and participation, the next three chapters explore specific criminal offences. All of the material discussed in the previous two chapters will continue to be relevant here.

Remember that whenever you discuss any criminal offence, you need to discuss what the *actus reus* and *mens rea* is. This could require you to discuss topics we looked at in Chapter 1. Depending on the wording of the offence, discussion of the *actus reus* could lead you to discuss the principles of causation, for example, whilst discussion of the *mens rea* could require you to discuss how the courts have interpreted the term 'intention'.

It is also possible that problem questions concerning particular offences may also require you to look at inchoate offences and accessory liability.

This chapter examines harm to the person that stops short of death. It discusses non-fatal offences against the person and sexual offences, focusing upon the offences in the Offences against the Person Act 1861 and the Sexual Offences Act 2003.

In relation to offences against the person, this chapter explores five general offences:

- assault

- battery

- assault occasioning actual bodily harm (abh) – s. 47 Offences against the Person Act 1861

- malicious wounding/inflicting grievous bodily harm – s. 20 Offences against the Person Act 1861

- malicious wounding/causing grievous bodily harm with intent – s. 18 Offences against the Person Act 1861

This list begins with the least serious and works its way down. In an answer to a problem question, you would usually work the other way around, starting with the most serious offence first.

This chapter also looks at the offences found in ss 23–24 of the Offences against the Person Act 1861 and the issue of consent. It then examines the main sexual offences found in the Sexual Offences Act 2003.

ASSAULT AND BATTERY

Actus reus

Assault and battery are separate summary offences.

The *actus reus* of an assault consists of causing the victim to apprehend immediate unlawful physical violence (*Logden v DPP* [1976]).

For many years, it was uncertain whether words alone could constitute an assault (*R v Meade and Belt* [1823]; *R v Wilson* [1955]). In *R v Burstow*; *R v Ireland* [1997], the House of Lords held that an assault could be committed by words alone, thus ending this longstanding uncertainty. The emphasis is now on the effect of the defendant's actions on the victim, rather than the means adopted by the defendant.

The *actus reus* of a battery consists of the actual infliction of unlawful physical violence. The degree of 'violence' required is minimal and can consist of the least touching of another (*Cole v Turner* [1705]).

Touching a person's clothing will amount to a battery, provided the contact is both unauthorised and capable of being felt by the victim (*R v Thomas* [1985]).

The courts presume that people impliedly consent to the normal touching that occurs in everyday life (*Collins v Wilcock* [1984]).

A battery can occur by indirect force where the defendant uses a weapon or other instrument to inflict physical harm on the victim, such as a car (*Fagan v MPC* [1968]).

Also a battery may be caused by the indirect use of force. In *Haystead v CC of Derbyshire* [2000] the defendant punched the victim causing the victim to drop a baby she was holding. The defendant was convicted of battery on the baby.

Mens rea

The *mens rea* for both assault and battery is intention or recklessness (*R v Savage* [1991]).

Statutory offences

The Divisional Court in *DPP v Little* [1992] found that not only were common assault and battery separate offences, but also that the Offences against the

Person Act 1861 had put them into a statutory form. It is, therefore, no longer correct to refer to them as common law assault and battery. They should now be charged under s 39 of the Criminal Justice Act 1988.

SECTION 47 OF THE OFFENCES AGAINST THE PERSON ACT 1861

Definition
Section 47 of the Offences against the Person Act 1861 provides that it is an offence to commit 'any assault occasioning actual bodily harm (abh)'.

Actus reus
An 'assault' within the meaning of s 47 can consist of either an assault in the technical sense of causing someone to fear immediate unlawful violence, or in the sense of a battery (that is, the infliction of unlawful violence).

'Occasioning' means the same as 'causing'; therefore, the rules relating to causation will be relevant (see Chapter 1).

Actual bodily harm was defined in *R v Miller* [1954] so as to include any hurt or injury likely to interfere with the health or comfort of the victim. Minor cuts and bruises may suffice, though it normally reflects more serious injuries, such as broken teeth, extensive bruising or cuts which require medical treatment. However, in *T v DPP* [2003] it was held that the victim's momentary loss of consciousness, following a kick to the head, could properly be regarded as actual bodily harm, even where there was no other discernible evidence of injury.

In *R v Chan-Fook* [1994], it was held that actual bodily harm includes psychiatric injury, but does not include mere emotions such as fear, distress or panic. The House of Lords, in *Burstow* [1997] and *Ireland* [1997], confirmed the decision in *Chan-Fook* by holding that recognisable psychiatric illness can amount to 'bodily harm' for the purposes of ss 47, 20 and 18 of the Offences against the Person Act 1861. In *DPP v Smith* [2006] it was held that actual bodily harm included cutting off a woman's pony tail because it was part of the body. In *R v Morris* [1997], the Court of Appeal held that where a defendant is on a charge of an assault occasioning actual bodily harm and the harm is alleged to have been occasioned by a non-physical assault, the case should not go to the jury without expert psychiatric evidence.

Mens rea

Only the *mens rea* for assault or battery needs to be proven.

There is no need to prove *mens rea* as to the actual bodily harm. All that needs to be proven is that the defendant intended or was reckless as to the assault or battery and that the assault and battery resulted in actual bodily harm. It is unnecessary to prove that the defendant intended or foresaw the risk of harm.

In *R v Savage* [1992] the defendant intended to throw the contents of a beer glass over the victim, but unintentionally the glass slipped from her hand and caused a wounding to the victim. It was held that a conviction under s 20 (see below) could not be sustained without the defendant foreseeing the possibility of injury, but a conviction for an offence under s 47 was possible because the defendant had the *mens rea* of an assault since she intended to throw the beer and this assault resulted in the victim's injury. For section 47 there was no need to show any *mens rea* as to the actual bodily harm. See also *R v Roberts* [1971].

▶ R v ROBERTS [1971]

For section 47 of the Offences against the Person Act 1861, there is no need to prove *mens rea* as to the actual bodily harm. The prosecution needs to prove the *mens rea* for assault or battery and that this caused the actual bodily harm.

Facts

The defendant ordered a passenger in his car to remove her clothes and began to pull at her coat. She jumped out of the moving car suffering concussion and grazing.

Held

The Court of Appeal held that the issue of actual bodily harm was simply a question of causation: it sufficed that it could be reasonably foreseen as a result of the assault or battery. There was no need to prove that the accused intended or was reckless in relation to the actual bodily harm.

SECTION 20 OF THE OFFENCES AGAINST THE PERSON ACT 1861

Definition

Section 20 creates two offences of 'malicious wounding' and 'maliciously inflicting grievous bodily harm' upon any other person.

Actus reus

A wounding requires a complete break of all the layers of the victim's skin (*JCC v Eisenhower* [1984]). Grievous bodily harm simply means 'serious harm' (*R v Saunders* [1985]).

Although most offences under s 20 will involve an assault, it was decided in *R v Wilson* [1983] that 'inflicting' does not necessarily imply an assault. It would seem that if 'inflicting' is to have any meaning at all it is to imply the need for causation. (See also *R v Burstow* [1997] where GBH, in the form of serious psychiatric injury, was inflicted by means of menacing telephone calls.)

Mens rea

The word 'malicious' implies a *mens rea* of intention or recklessness.

The decision of the court in *R v Mowatt* [1967] placed a 'gloss' on the *Cunningham* definition of recklessness in relation to s 20 in that the defendant must be shown to have been aware of the possibility of causing the victim *some physical harm*, albeit not serious harm.

As such foresight that the victim will be frightened is insufficient to find liability in relation to s 20; as stated above, the defendant must have foreseen some physical harm, if only of a minor character (*R v Sullivan* [1984]).

SECTION 18 OF THE OFFENCES AGAINST THE PERSON ACT 1861

Definition

By s 18, it is an offence to 'maliciously ... wound or cause any grievous bodily harm ... with intent to do some grievous bodily harm'.

Actus reus

The *actus reus* is wounding or causing grievous bodily harm to any person. This is the same as under s 20 but for two differences.

Firstly, the injuries may be 'to any person' (as opposed 'to any other person'). This suggests that wounding or causing on yourself is only covered by s 18. Secondly, the grievous bodily harm is caused rather than inflicted. Normal rules of causation therefore apply.

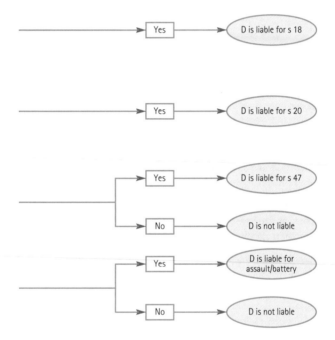

Mens rea

There are two elements to the *mens rea*.

The first element is the same as s 20. The defendant must have 'maliciously' wounded or 'maliciously' caused grievous bodily harm. As we have seen, the word 'malicious' has now been interpreted as requiring intention or recklessness.

The second element is that in addition the defendant must either intend to do some grievous bodily harm to any person or to resist or prevent the lawful apprehension. The difference between s 18 and s 20 is therefore that s 20 requires intention (*R v Belfon* [1976]). This may be either direct or oblique intent (*R v Bryson* [1985]).

Racially and religiously aggravated assaults

These aggravated features were added by the Crime and Disorder Act 1998. Section 29 states that it is an offence if a person commits a common assault, s 47 or s 20 offence which is racially or religiously aggravated. If a defendant is convicted of this offence the maximum penalties they face are higher than the non-aggravated offences.

SUMMARY OF NON-FATAL OFFENCES

SECTIONS 23 AND 24 OF THE OFFENCES AGAINST THE PERSON ACT 1861

Actus reus

Both ss 23 and 24 require the administration of a noxious substance. Whether or not a substance is noxious will depend upon the circumstances in which it is taken. Such circumstances include the quality and quantity of the substance as well as the characteristics of the person to whom it is given (*R v Marcus* [1981]).

'Administering' means causing to be taken, for example, by spraying CS gas into someone's face (*R v Gillard* [1988]).

The *actus reus* of s 23 requires that life must be endangered or grievous bodily harm inflicted as a consequence of the administration of the noxious substance.

Mens rea

Both offences require that the noxious substance be administered intentionally or recklessly. In addition, s 24 requires proof of an intent to injure, aggrieve or annoy the victim.

CONSENT

The general rule is that the victim's consent may be a defence to a charge of assault or battery but is not a defence to offences under s 47, s 20 and s 18.

Consent will only be a defence if:

(a) The victim did consent (either expressly or impliedly).

As we have seen, it is presumed that people impliedly consent to normal touching that occurs as part of everyday life (*Collins v Wilcock* [1984]).

Previously it was thought that if the victim consented to an act then they also consented to any incidental risk of injury and illness resulting from that act. However, the Court of Appeal decision in *R v Dica* [2004] shows that this is no longer the case. The victim had consented to unprotected sex but was not aware that the defendant was HIV positive. The Court of Appeal held that the victim did not impliedly consent to the risk of infection.

(b) The victim was capable of giving informed consent.

Some victims may be incapable of giving consent (due to a mental disorder, learning difficulty or age). Moreover a victim cannot be said to consent unless they have some knowledge of the nature of what they are consenting to: *R v Konzani* [2005].

In *R v Tabassum* [2000] the defendant examined three women's breasts under the pretence of carrying out a study on breast cancer. The Court of Appeal held that they had not consented. They had only consented to touching for a medical purpose: 'there was consent as to the nature of the act but not its quality'.

(c) The act was one to which the victim could consent.

In *AG's Reference (No 6 of 1980)* [1981] it was held that: 'It is not in the public interest that people should try to cause or should cause each other actual bodily harm for no good reason .... this means that most fights will be unlawful regardless of consent.'

However, it was noted that there were exceptions to this rule: 'properly conducted games and sports, lawful chastisement or correction, reasonable surgical interference, dangerous exhibitions etc.'

In *R v Brown* [1994] the House of Lords said that good public policy reasons would be needed before a new exempt category would be recognised. They held that consent was not a defence where A wounds or assaults B occasioning actual bodily harm in the course of a sado-masochistic encounter.

In *R v Wilson* [1996] the Court of Appeal suggested that the question should be 'does public policy or the public interest demand that the appellant's activity should be vested by the sanctions of the criminal law'. Consent was an answer to a charge made against a man who burned his wife's buttocks with a hot knife at her request to brand his initials.

SEXUAL OFFENCES

The Sexual Offences Act 2003 repealed almost all of the Sexual Offences Acts 1956 and 1967, the Indecency with Children Act 1960, and the Sex Offenders Act 1997. In their place it establishes a new law of rape and sexual assault, a new raft of sexual offences against vulnerable persons (children and the mentally disabled), a dramatically expanded range of offences dealing with prostitution, child pornography, sexual trafficking, and a number of completely new offences, including new crimes of voyeurism and 'grooming'.

The first four sections create four non-consensual crimes: rape (s 1), assault by penetration (s 2), sexual assault (s 3) and causing sexual activity without consent (s 4).

All four offences take a similar form:

Actus reus = (1) do relevant act + (2) no consent
Mens rea = (1) intend relevant act + (2) no reasonable belief that victim consented

The main thing that differs is the relevant act. Put simply:

- for rape, the relevant act is the penetration of vagina, anus or mouth by penis without consent;

- for assault by penetration, the relevant act is the penetration of vagina or anus by anything else (if sexual) without consent;

- for sexual assault the relevant act is touching (if sexual) without consent;

- for s 4 the relevant act is causing sexual activity without consent.

(1) RAPE

The offence of rape is defined in s 1 of the Sexual Offences Act (SOA) 2003.

Actus reus

The actus reus is the penetration by penis of vagina, anus or mouth without consent.

The offence of rape can only be committed by a man as a principal offender (a woman or a man can be an accomplice to rape). It is an offence for a man to rape a woman or a man. The *actus reus* of the offence requires evidence of penile penetration of vagina, anus *or* mouth. There is no need to prove ejaculation.

Unlike those offences to which consent can be raised as a defence, rape requires the prosecution to prove the absence of consent as part of the *actus reus* of the offence. The significance of this is that the absence of consent has to be proved beyond reasonable doubt.

The SOA 2003 provides a limited definition of consent – 'a person consents if he agrees by choice, and has the freedom and capacity to make that choice' (s 74). This definition connotes a free, genuine and subsisting agreement, express or implied, to the act of sexual intercourse. So an agreement obtained by duress, not being a free agreement, does not amount to the 'consent' required. An agreement founded on the victim being mistaken or deceived as to the identity of the defendant, or as to the nature of the act, is not the 'consent' required, because it is not a genuine agreement. In *R v B* [2006] a defendant did not disclose to the complainant that he was HIV positive. He was not liable for rape as they had consensual sexual intercourse despite his non-disclosure.

In a further controversial development, the SOA 2003 introduces sets of presumptions about the absence of consent. The presumptions come in two forms:

▦ Rebuttable presumptions (s 75)

If it is proved that the defendant did the relevant act and one of the following circumstances existed at the time:

- ● violence was used against the complainant or the complainant was put in fear of immediate violence;

- the complainant was made to fear that violence was being used or would be used on another person (eg threats of violence towards complainant's child);

- the complainant was being unlawfully detained;

- the complainant was asleep;

- because of the complainant's disability, they would not have been able to communicate consent;

- a substance was administered to the complainant, without their consent, which was capable of causing the complainant to be stupefied or overpowered at the time of the relevant act,

it will be presumed that:

(a) the complainant did not consent to the act, and

(b) the defendant did not reasonably believe that the complainant consented,

unless the defendant adduces sufficient evidence to raise an issue to the contrary.

Conclusive presumptions (s 76)

The same presumptions will be also made if one of the following circumstances existed at the time:

- the defendant intentionally deceived the complainant as to the nature or purpose of the relevant act;

- the defendant intentionally induced the complainant to consent to the relevant act by impersonating a person known personally to the complainant.

But in these circumstances the presumptions will be conclusive: the defendant will have no opportunity to rebut them.

When determining the issue of consent under the SOA 2003, work backwards through sections 74–76. First, look to see if D's act means that there is a conclusive presumption under s 76. If not, then look to see if there is an evidential presumption under s 75. And where there is not, fall back on the general definition under s 74.

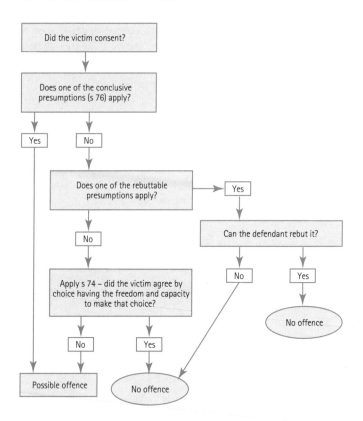

Mens rea

The prosecution must show that the defendant intended to have sexual intercourse and that he did not *reasonably* believe that the victim was consenting (s 1(1)(c)). In determining the issue of consent, reference should be made to sections 74–76 (as discussed above).

In other words, where the defendant claims he believed that the victim was consenting, if such a belief, though honestly held, is proved to be unreasonable, the jury should convict. In deciding whether the defendant's belief was unreasonable, the jury should have regard to all the circumstances, including any steps the defendant could reasonably have been expected to take to ascertain whether the victim consented (s 1(2)). This latter provision places an onus on the defendant to ascertain whether or not there is consent in situations where there might be doubt. As a whole, the burden on the Crown has clearly been lessened in that even if it cannot negative an honest belief that the victim was consenting, it may be able to show that that belief was unreasonable.

Sections 1–4

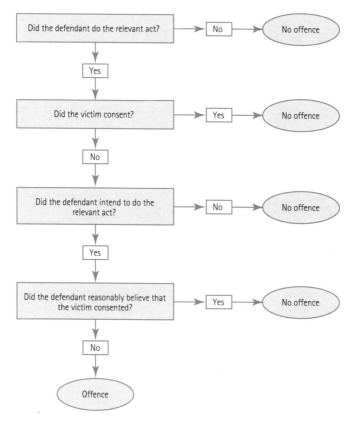

OTHER NON-CONSENSUAL OFFENCES

In relation to the other 'non-consensual' offences (namely assault by penetration (s 2), sexual assault (s 3) and causing a person to engage in sexual activity without consent (s 4)), the requirement that belief in consent is reasonable and the test as to what is reasonable, is the same as applies in relation to rape (s 1). Similarly, the rebuttable and conclusive presumptions as to consent and general definition of consent also apply. In short, it is only the relevant act which differs.

(2) ASSAULT BY PENETRATION

Section 2 covers assaults that involve penetration of the vagina or anus with objects or body parts other than the penis, or where the victim is not sure what was used to penetrate them. The penetration must be sexual so that it excludes, for example, intimate searches and medical procedures. Section 78 provides that an activity is 'sexual' if a 'reasonable' person would view it as such having regard to the nature of the act and where necessary to the circumstances and/or the purpose of any person in relation to the activity.

It must be proved that the penetration was intentional, that the victim did not consent to the penetration and that the defendant did not reasonably believe that the victim consented. This offence can be committed by a male or female, against a male or female. Assault by penetration and sexual assault together replace the old statutory offence of indecent assault.

(3) SEXUAL ASSAULT

Section 3 makes it an offence for the defendant intentionally to touch another person sexually without that person's consent, provided that the defendant does not reasonably believe that there is consent. This offence is intended to capture all other non-penetrative behaviour previously caught by the offence of indecent assault. 'Touching' is defined in the Act (s 79) so as to include touching (a) with any part of the body, (b) with anything else, (c) through anything, and includes touching amounting to penetration. This offence can be committed by a male or female, against a male or female.

(4) CAUSING A PERSON TO ENGAGE IN SEXUAL ACTIVITY WITHOUT CONSENT

Section 4 makes it an offence for a defendant intentionally to cause another person to engage in sexual activity without that person's consent. As above, if the defendant contends that he believed there was consent, the Crown must prove that he had no such belief, or, if he had, that his belief was unreasonable in the circumstances. This provision was intended to close a perceived gap in the law to allow the prosecution of someone who forces another person to perform sexual or indecent acts against their will. It covers, for example, cases where women force men to have sex with them, when A forces B to have sex with C and where A forces B to perform a sexual act on themselves or with an animal. This offence can be committed by a male or female, against a male or female.

CHILD SEX OFFENCES

In addition to the four general non-consensual crimes, the Sexual Offences Act 2003 also creates specific offences against children. In relation to these crimes, the consent of the child is irrelevant.

Sections 5 to 8 only apply to where the victim is under 13. They take the following form:

Actus reus = (1) do relevant act + (2) victim is under 13

Mens rea = (1) intend relevant act

There is strict liability in relation to the second part of the *actus reus*, the age of the victim.

This applies to the following offences:

- rape of a child under 13 (s 5);

- assault of a child under 13 by penetration (s 6);

- sexual assault of a child under 13 (s 7);

- causing or inciting a child under 13 to engage in sexual activity (s 8).

Sections 5–8

Sections 9 to 15 create further child sex offences which apply where the victim is under 16. They take the following form:

> *Actus reus* = (1) do relevant act + (2) victim is under 16
>
> *Mens rea* = (1) intend relevant act + (2) no reasonable belief that victim was over 16

However, ss 9 to 15 can also be charged in relation to children under s 13. Where they are, they take the same format as the specific offences under ss 5–8:

> *Actus reus* = (1) do relevant act + (2) victim is under 13
>
> *Mens rea* = (1) intend relevant act

This applies to the following offences:

- sexual activity with a child (s 9);
- causing or inciting a child to engage in sexual activity (s 10);

- engaging in sexual activity in the presence of a child (s 11);

- causing a child to watch a sexual act (s 12);

- arranging or facilitating commission of a child sex offence (s 14);

- meeting a child following sexual grooming, etc (s 15).

Where the defendant is aged under 18, the courts are permitted to grant a shorter sentence (s 13).

Sections 9–15

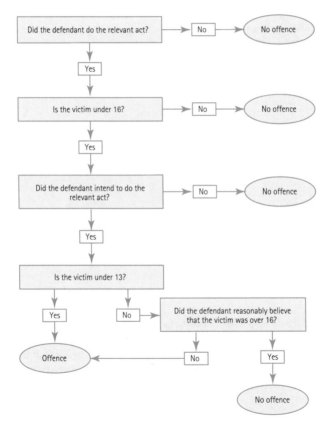

OTHER OFFENCES AND PROVISIONS UNDER THE SEXUAL OFFENCES ACT 2003

The Act also covers offences involving an abuse of a position of trust towards a child, familial child sex offences, offences designed to give protection to persons with a mental disorder or a learning disability, offences relating to prostitution, child pornography, and trafficking. It provides for preparatory offences, such as administering a substance with intent to commit a sexual offence, and a number of miscellaneous offences, such as voyeurism and intercourse with an animal. There is provision for extra-territorial jurisdiction for most of the offences contained in the Act if committed against a child under 16.

Part 2 of the Act contains extensive provisions relating to registration and notification obligations imposed on sex offenders.

You should now be confident that you would be able to tick all of the boxes on the checklist at the beginning of this chapter. To check your knowledge of Non-fatal offences against the person why not visit the companion website and take the Multiple Choice Question test. Check your understanding of the terms and vocabulary used in this chapter with the flashcard glossary.

4

Fatal offences

Homicide

Murder

Manslaughter

Loss of control

Diminished responsibility

Constructive manslaughter

Gross negligence manslaughter

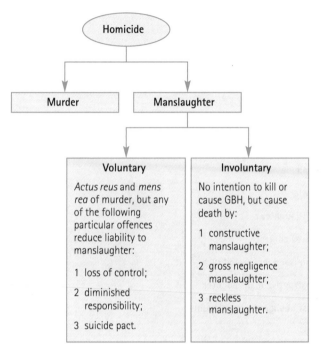

HOMICIDE

Murder and manslaughter share a common *actus reus*. You need to keep your eye on the *mens rea*.

If the defendant has fulfilled the *actus reus* and *mens rea* of murder then on the face of it they are liable for murder. The only reason why they may not be so liable is if one of the partial defences applies. The partial defences are loss of control, diminished responsibility and suicide pacts. If one of these applies then the defendant is liable for voluntary manslaughter.

If the defendant has fulfilled the *actus reus* but does **not** have the *mens rea* of murder then they cannot be liable for murder. The only homicide offence that can apply is involuntary manslaughter. There are three types: illegal and dangerous act, gross negligence, subjective recklessness.

You also need to be aware of the offence of infanticide.

Actus reus + *mens rea* = murder
Actus reus + *mens rea* + partial defence = voluntary manslaughter Three partial defences: provocation, diminished responsibility and suicide pacts
Actus reus – *mens rea* = potentially involuntary manslaughter Three types: illegal and dangerous act, gross negligence, subjective recklessness

The Law Commission (2006) has advocated widespread reform of homicide. The then government decided to implement this reform on a piecemeal basis. Reform of the partial defences was made by the Coroners and Justice Act 2009.

MURDER

Actus reus

The *actus reus* of murder was defined by Coke (1797) as the unlawful killing of any reasonable creature under the King's peace. This excludes foetuses and alien enemies in time of war. An enemy alien is under the Queen's Peace if they are a prisoner of war.

In more modern language, it may be said that the *actus reus* of murder is causing the unlawful death of a human being. The normal rules of causation apply. There must be both [a] factual causation and [b] legal causation (see Chapter 1).

A patient kept alive on a life support machine is not regarded as legally dead and is, therefore, capable of being murdered. The original attacker will be held to have caused death if the machine is turned off as a result of a medical decision made in good faith (*R v Malcherek and Steel* [1981]).

The law of homicide protects the newborn child once it becomes capable of independent existence from the mother, and this includes a conjoined twin who is totally dependent on its twin for oxygenated blood (*Re A (Children) (Conjoined twins: surgical separation)* [2001]). There is no need for the umbilical cord to have been cut (*R v Reeves* [1839]), but the child must have been totally expelled from the mother's womb (*R v Poulton* [1832]).

Mens rea

The necessary *mens rea* for murder is an intention to kill or cause grievous bodily harm (*R v Vickers* [1957]).

In cases where it is not clear whether the defendant had such an intention, the jury must consider the evidence of what the defendant actually foresaw, and the more evidence there is that he foresaw death or grievous bodily harm as a consequence of his actions, the stronger the inference that he intended to kill (*R v Hancock and Shankland* [1986]).

In *R v Nedrick* [1986], the court supplemented the decision in *Hancock* by suggesting that the jury must be satisfied that the defendant foresaw death or grievous bodily harm as a virtual certainty before they could infer intention. The House of Lords, in *R v Woollin* [1998], confirmed the approach of the Court of Appeal in *Nedrick*, with the small modification that the more logical and simpler word 'find' should be used instead of 'infer'.

▶ R V WOOLLIN [1998]

Where a harm was the virtually certain result of the defendant's actions and the defendant appreciated such, a jury can find intention.

Facts

Woollin was convicted of murder after losing his temper and shaking his baby son and throwing him on a hard surface. The trial judge did not use the trial direction provided by *Nedrick* [1986].

Held

Intention can only be found where the jury are satisfied that the harm caused was a virtually certain consequence of the defendant's actions which the defendant appreciated.

Where the defendant's foresight of the harm was anything less than virtual certainty, they would lack intention.

MANSLAUGHTER

VOLUNTARY MANSLAUGHTER

The category of voluntary manslaughter covers those cases where mitigating circumstances reduces the conviction from murder to manslaughter.

There are three partial defences loss of control, diminished responsibility and suicide pact. The successful plea of these partial defences does not not exonerate the defendant but serves to reduces conviction from murder to manslaughter (and hence avoids mandatory sentence of life imprisonment).

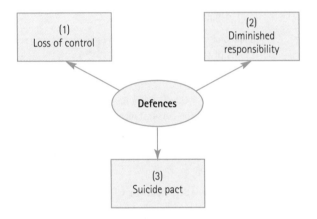

These partial defences are only available on a charge of murder but they may be a mitigating factor at sentence for other offences.

In order for the partial defences to apply, the prosecution must prove that the defendant has committed all the elements of a murder: they must prove that the defendant has caused death of another person unlawfully (*actus reus*) with the intention to kill or cause grievous bodily harm (the *mens rea*).

The Coroners and Justice Act 2009 has reformed diminished responsibility and has replaced the old partial defence of provocation with a new but similar partial defence of loss of control. At time of writing, the extent to which the old case law continues to apply is unknown. You should therefore be able to compare and contrast the law on voluntary manslaughter before and after the enactment of the Coroners and Justice Act 2009.

(1) LOSS OF CONTROL

Prior to the Coroners and Justice Act 2009, provocation was recognised as mitigating factor in murder that would reduce an intentional killing to manslaughter. The partial defence could be found in section 3 of the Homicide Act 1957 which expanded on the common law defence as defined by Devlin J in *R v Duffy* [1949].

The new partial defence of loss of control is to be found in sections 54 and 55 of the Coroners and Justice Act 2009. Section 54(1) reads:

(1)   Where a person ('D') kills or is a party to the killing of another ('V'), D is not to be convicted of murder if—

   (a)   D's acts and omissions in doing or being a party to the killing resulted from D's **loss of self-control**,

   (b)   the loss of self-control had a **qualifying trigger**, and

   (c)   a person of D's sex and age, with a normal degree of tolerance and self-restraint and in the **circumstances** of D, might have reacted in the same or in a similar way to D.

The emboldened words highlight the three criteria that need to be met in order for the partial defence to apply:

1. The subjective test – did the defendant lose self-control?

2. The cause: the loss of control must have had a qualifying trigger.

3. The objective test – would the reasonable person have lost self-control?

Note that the prosecution are required to prove all the elements of murder *and* to disprove the provocation. Section 54(5)–(6) of the Coroners and Justice Act 2009 state that it is a matter of law for the judge to decide whether sufficient evidence has been raised to leave the partial defence to the jury. This tightens up the partial defence since under the old law on provocation, the rule was that where there was evidence of provocation then this had to be left to the jury (*R v Cambridge* [1994]).

The subjective test – did the defendant lose self-control?

Under the old partial defence of provocation, it needed to be proved that there had been a sudden and temporary loss of control, rendering the accused so subject to passion as to make him or her for the moment not master of his mind (*R v Ibrams* [1981]). For example, the defence failed in *R v Ibrams* [1981] where the defendant had been bullied and terrorised over a period but the last occasion of provocation was seven days before the planned fatal attack.

The defence was denied if the defendant had regained his self-control before killing the victim. Premeditated calculated killings were therefore denied the defence since evidence of a plan indicates that there was no loss of self-control.

Section 54(2) of the Coroners and Justice Act 2010 makes it clear that the loss of control does not need to be sudden. This seems to reverse the old law. However, s 54(4) says that the defence does not apply where 'D acted in a considered desire for revenge'.

This suggests that it remains open for the judge and the jury to take into account any delay between a relevant incident and the killing in order to determine whether the killing occurred whilst the defendant lost self-control.

The jury are entitled to look beyond the immediate act and to take into account the relevant background. The final instance could be relatively minor but could be regarded as 'the straw that breaks the camel's back'. However, there must still be evidence that the defendant did actually lose self-control at the time of the killing (*R v Humphreys* [1995] and *R v Thornton (No 2)* [1996]).

The cause: the loss of control must have had a qualifying trigger

Under s 3 of the Homicide Act 1957, there was little legal restriction on what could cause provocation. The Act simply required that the defendant was provoked 'whether by things done or by things said or by both together'. In *R v Doughty* [1986] the Court of Appeal held that a baby's crying could amount to provocation.

The new partial defence seeks to limit the broadness of the old law by stating that the loss of control must be attributable to one of two qualifying triggers laid out in s 55(3)–(4). Section 55(5) provides that D's loss of self-control can be 'attributable to a combination of the matters mentioned in subsections (3) and (4)'.

The first qualifying trigger, found in s 55(3), applies where the defendant's loss of self-control was attributable to the defendant's fear of 'serious violence' from the victim against the defendant or another identified person. Note that only the fear of serious violence is needed, it does not need to be shown that there was violence. The word 'serious' suggests that fear of minor acts of violence or damage to property will not suffice.

Section 56(6)(a) provides that if the defendant incites the violence for the purpose of providing an excuse then he cannot rely on fear of that violence for the partial defence. So, if the defendant says 'go on punch me in the face', hoping that they would, then that does not count as 'fear of serious violence'.

The second qualifying trigger, found in s 55(4), applies where the defendant's loss of self-control was attributable to a thing or things done or said (or both). However, unlike the old law of provocation, s 55(4) stipulates that this qualifying trigger will apply only if the things done or said 'constituted circumstances of an extremely grave character' and 'caused D to have a justifiable sense of being seriously wronged'.

It is not clear what these terms mean. It is clear that circumstances alone will not suffice. The reference to 'circumstances of an extremely grave character' seems to suggest that the circumstances must be unusual and very serious. Whether the defendant has 'a justifiable sense of being seriously wronged' is an objective question for a jury to determine.

Section 56(6)(b) provides that if the defendant incites the thing done or said then he cannot rely on fear of that violence for the partial defence. Section 56(6)(c) provides that sexual infidelity can never be the ground for this trigger. A defendant who killed an unfaithful partner cannot blame the victim for what occurred.

The objective test – would the reasonable person have lost self-control?
Like the old defence of provocation, the partial defence of loss of control also has an objective element: put simply, would the reasonable person do as the defendant did?

The question which proved problematic for the courts was which, if any, of the characteristics of the defendant should be attributed to the reasonable person. Prior to the Homicide Act 1957, the reasonable person was not individualised at all. If the defendant killed the victim after being provoked by taunts about his impotence, the jury were asked to consider the taunts on a reasonable person who was not impotent (*DPP v Bedder* [1954]). This was often considered unfair. After all a taunt of impotence is quite different if you are indeed impotent.

In *DPP v Camplin* [1978], it was held that the Homicide Act 1957 had changed the law. There now existed a distinction between factors that affect the gravity of the provocation and those which simply affect the defendant's power of self-control.

Factors that affect the gravity of the provocation are those characteristics of the defendant that mean that the taunt hurts them more than other people. These factors are always attributed to the reasonable person. So, if the victim taunted the impotent defendant about his impotence, then the test that is applied is whether the reasonable person who was impotent would have done as the defendant did.

Factors which affect the defendant's power of self-control are those characteristics of the defendant that may render them more likely to attack but which is not mentioned in the taunt itself. *DPP v Camplin* [1978] provided that age and sex were the only factors affecting the defendant's power of self-control that should be taken into account.

However, following *DPP v Camplin* [1978], a number of decisions in the Court of Appeal sought to take a broader approach as to what factors affecting the defendant's power of self control could be attributed (see *R v Ahluwalia* [1992]; *R v Dryden* [1995]; *R v Humphreys* [1995]). Although the Privy Council decision, *Luc Thiet Thuan v R* [1996], criticised this gradual erosion of the objective requirement, the House of Lords in *R v Smith (Morgan)* [2001] preferred the broad view that individual peculiarities which reduced the defendant's level of self-control could be taken into account.

The narrower test from *DPP v Camplin* [1978], however, found favour in the Privy Council case of *Attorney General for Jersey v Holley* [2005] in which an enlarged board of nine Law Lords held on a majority of six to three that the majority decision in *Smith* had been erroneous. The Court of Appeal ruled in *R v James and Karimi* [2006] that the Privy Council in *Holley* was good law and followed that rather than the House of Lords in *Smith*.

It seems likely that the objective test found in the Coroners and Justice Act 2009 follows the narrower approach found in *DPP v Camplin* [1978] and *Attorney General for Jersey v Holley* [2005]. However, the wording of the objective test is somewhat unclear and so its meaning will not become clear until there are reported cases on the new law.

According to s 54(1)(a), the partial defence will only apply if 'a person of the defendant's sex and age with a normal degree of tolerance and self-restraint and in the same circumstances as the defendant, must have reacted in a similar way'.

Unlike the old law, there is no reference to 'reasonable person'. Instead, the comparator is a person with a normal degree of tolerance and self-restraint and in the circumstances of D'. The reference to circumstances makes it clear that the background to the loss of control can be taken into account. But 'circumstances' is limited by s 54(3) which states that:

> the reference to 'the circumstances of D' is a reference to all of D's circumstances other than those whose only relevance to D's conduct is that they bear on D's general capacity for tolerance or self-restraint.

This seems to suggest that the defendant's general characteristics that do not affect the gravity of the provocation are excluded. The fact that the defendant was generally intolerant or irritable or excessively jealous or had anger issues would be ignored unless this was the subject of the taunt.

The Act therefore seems to codify the restrictive view found in *DPP v Camplin* [1978] and *Attorney General for Jersey v Holley* [2005]: the age and sex of the victim and factors affecting the gravity of the provocation are taken into account, but factors that simply relate to the defendant's general capacity for tolerance or self-restraint are not.

Loss of Self-Control: The Three Steps	[1] There is a sudden and temporary loss of self-control . . . . . .
	[2] Caused by a qualifying trigger . . . and
	[3] A person of the same age and sex as the defendant would have also lost his self-control

(2) DIMINISHED RESPONSIBILITY

Unlike loss of control, the partial defence of diminished responsibility can still be found in s 2 of the Homicide Act 1957. However, s 52 of the Coroners and Justice Act 2009 has substituted a revised version of s 2 into the 1957 Act.

Section 2(1) of the Homicide Act 1957, as amended, provides:

(1) A person ('D') who kills or is a party to the killing of another is not to be convicted of murder if D was suffering from an abnormality of mental functioning which—

    (a) arose from a recognised medical condition,

    (b) substantially impaired D's ability to do one or more of the things mentioned in subsection (1A), and

    (c) provides an explanation for D's acts and omissions in doing or being a party to the killing.

Under the new law, there are four tests:

(i) The defendant must suffer from an abnormality of mental functioning.

(ii) The cause of the abnormality must be from a recognised medical condition.

(iii) The effect must be to substantially impair one of more of the things listed in 1A.

(iv) The abnormality must cause, or be a significant contributory factor in causing the defendant to kill.

The burden is on the defendant to prove the defence on the balance of probabilities (*R v Dunbar* [1957]).

The defendant must suffer from an abnormality of mental functioning

This replaces the reference in the old law to an 'abnormality of mind'. In *R v Byrne* [1960], Lord Parker CJ defined abnormality of mind as 'a state of mind that the reasonable person would find abnormal'. The case of Byrne, a sexual psychopath who found it difficult to control his perverted desires, came within s 2. This is considerably wider than the 'defect of reason' under the *M'Naghten* rules (see insanity in Chapter 6). If it is established that the defendant has abnormality of the mind, it must also be shown that such abnormality impaired his 'mental responsibility'.

The reference to an 'abnormality of the mind' was long criticised on the basis that it was not a psychiatric term. However, the new phrase 'abnormality of mental functioning' is also not a psychiatric term. The term 'mental functioning' is left undefined. It will be up to the courts to determine whether the new term has a different meaning

The cause of the abnormality: must be from a recognised medical condition

This is more precise and scientific than the old law which required the abnormality to arise 'from a condition of arrested or retarded development of mind or any inherent causes or induced by disease or injury'. These terms were never defined satisfactory by the courts; however, in practice it was understood to require a medical condition.

Does alcoholism found a defence within s 2? This was considered in *R v Tandy* [1989]. An alcoholic strangled her 11-year-old daughter after drinking a bottle of vodka and upon hearing that the daughter had been sexually abused. The Court of Appeal upheld her conviction for murder, and in doing so they indicated that the defence based on alcoholism was only available where the craving was such as to make the consumption of drink or drugs involuntary. An alcoholic's irresistible craving for alcohol can amount to an abnormality.

Where a defendant seeks to rely on an abnormality of the mind other than alcoholism (eg clinical depression) to establish a defence under s 2, but is intoxicated at the time of the killing, it had previously been thought that the defendant had to show that he would have killed even if he had been sober before he could rely on the defence (*R v Atkinson* [1985]). This was overruled by the House of Lords in *R v Dietschmann* [2003] and it is now established that the defendant's abnormality is not required to be the sole cause of the conduct. The Lords ruled that where a defendant is intoxicated at the time of the killing and seeks to prove diminished responsibility on the basis of an abnormality of the mind other than alcoholism, he need only show that his abnormality of mind substantially impaired his mental responsibility. It does not matter that intoxication was an additional contributory factor or that he may not have killed without being drunk.

In *R v Stewart* [2009], the trial judge gave a direction saying that the defence was to be denied if the jury found that any of the defendant's drinking was voluntary. The Court of Appeal held that this was a misdirection.

The jury should be directed to consider all the evidence, including the opinions of medical experts. The issues likely to arise in this kind of case and on which they should form their own judgment will include:

(a) The extent and seriousness of the defendant's dependency on alcohol.

(b) The extent to which the defendant can control his drinking or to chose whether to drink or not was reduced.

(c) Whether he was capable of abstinence for alcohol.

(d) If so, for how long.

(e) Whether he was drinking for some particular reason.

The effect must be to substantially impair one or more of the things listed in 1A

The word 'substantially' has been retained from the old definition. 'Substantial' was understood as meaning that the impairment need not be 'total' but must be more than 'trivial' or 'minimal' (*R v Egan* [1993]).

However, now rather than just proving that they impair mental responsibility, it will need to be proven to affect one or more of the three things listed in 1A

(1A) Those things are—

(a) to understand the nature of D's conduct;

(b) to form a rational judgment;

(c) to exercise self-control.

The abnormality must cause, or be a significant contributory factor in causing the defendant to kill

This fourth test seems to be new. The then Government insisted that a stronger causal requirement was necessary. A link between the abnormality and the killing must be shown. The abnormality must be the 'explanation'.

However, in practice, was this the law anyway? For instance, the Judicial Studies Board Specimen Direction on diminished responsibility stated that:

> Substantially impaired means just that. You must conclude that his abnormality of mind was *a real cause* of the defendant's conduct. The defendant need not prove that his condition was the sole cause of it, but he must show that it was more than merely a trivial one.

Diminished Responsibility: The Four Steps	[1] An abnormality of mental functioning ...
	[2] Arising from disease medical condition ...
	[3] Which substantially impaired the defendant's responsibility to do one or more of the three things in 1A
	[4] Which causes or is a significant contributing factor in causing the defendant to kill.

(3) SUICIDE PACT

Section 4 of the Homicide Act 1957 provides that any killing carried out in pursuance of a suicide pact will be treated as manslaughter, rather than as murder.

INFANTICIDE

Section 1(1) of the Infanticide Act 1938 provides that where a woman kills her child before it reaches the age of 12 months and there is evidence to show that at the time of the killing the balance of her mind was disturbed by the effect of giving birth, then the jury is entitled to find her guilty of infanticide rather than murder.

INVOLUNTARY MANSLAUGHTER

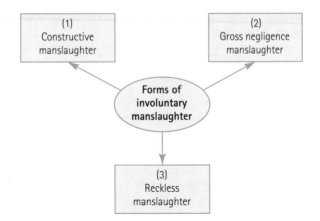

A person is guilty of involuntary manslaughter where although he has fulfilled the *actus reus* of murder, he kills without the needed *mens rea* of murder.

If he has a lesser fault element which is recognised by the common law as sufficient to found liability for homicide then he is liable for involuntary manslaughter. Three categories are so recognised: constructive, gross negligence and recklessness manslaughter. Note that constructive manslaughter is also known as unlawful and dangerous act manslaughter.

(1) CONSTRUCTIVE MANSLAUGHTER

This offence requires proof that the defendant intentionally committed a dangerous criminal act which resulted in the death of the victim. *DPP v Newbury and Jones* [1976] confirmed the four elements of the offence as:

(a) defendant did an act with the intention to do so;

(b) the act was criminally unlawful;

(c) the act was dangerous; and

(d) the act caused the victim's death.

The objective nature of the 'dangerous' act was established in *R v Church* [1966], where it was said that:

> ... the unlawful act must be such as all sober and reasonable people would inevitably recognise must subject the other person to, at least, the risk of some harm resulting therefrom, albeit not serious harm ...

What is meant by 'harm' in this context was clarified in *R v Dawson* [1985], where it was held that the jury must be directed to consider the possibility of *physical* harm as opposed to mere emotional disturbance.

Moreover, the reasonable person should be endowed with all the knowledge that the defendant has gained in the course of the crime (*R v Watson* [1989]).

The illegal act required for constructive manslaughter must be a criminal act (*R v Franklin* [1883]), but there is no need for the act to be 'aimed' at the victim. For example, in *R v Goodfellow* [1986] the defendant, wishing to be rehoused, set fire to his council house. The fire spread faster than he expected, killing his wife, child, and another person. The Court of Appeal upheld the conviction for manslaughter, even though the defendant's acts were not directed at the victims but rather against property.

In terms of causing the victim's death, the normal rules of causation apply (see Chapter 1). In *R v Kennedy* [2007] the House of Lords confirmed that legal chain of causation is broken where the victim is an informed adult of sound mind and their actions are free, deliberate and informed.

The certified question for the House of Lords was 'When is it appropriate to find someone guilty of manslaughter where the person has been involved in the supply of a class A controlled drug, which is then freely and voluntarily self-administered by the person to whom it was supplied, and the administration of the drug then causes his death?' Their Lordship's answer was in the case of a fully informed adult, never. All that is required for the *mens rea* is an intention to do such an act; it is not necessary for the defendant to know that the act is criminal or dangerous (*DPP v Newbury and Jones* [1976]).

(2) GROSS NEGLIGENCE MANSLAUGHTER

Following the decision of the House of Lords in *R v Adomako* [1994], to establish this form of manslaughter the prosecution must prove:

▩ *A duty of care*

There must be a duty of care under the ordinary principles of negligence, as developed in the law of tort. A duty of care is typically imposed by a family or professional relationship. However, the Court of Appeal in *R v Evans* [2009] controversially applied the 'duty' theory from *R v Miller* [1983] (see Chapter 1) in the context of gross negligent manslaughter.

▩ *Breach of that duty*

The duty may be breached whenever there is a reasonably foreseeable risk of injury to health occurring (*R v Stone and Dobinson* [1977]).

▩ *Gross negligence*

According to the Court of Appeal in *R v Prentice and Others* [1993], a decision confirmed by the House of Lords in *R v Adomako*, any of the following states of mind could lead a jury to make a finding of gross negligence:

(a) indifference to an obvious risk of injury to health;

(b) actual foresight of the risk coupled with the determination nevertheless to run it;

(c) an appreciation of the risk coupled with an intention to avoid it, but also coupled with such a high degree of negligence in the attempted avoidance as the jury considers justifies conviction;

(d) inattention or failure to advert to a serious risk which goes beyond 'mere inadvertence' in respect of an obvious and important matter which the defendant's duty demanded he should address.

Two of the above four types of gross negligence, (a) and (b), seem to be subjective mental states (in relation to (a), surely, you can only be *indifferent* to a result which is foreseen?), whereas (c) and (d) are clearly objective mental states. However, each case, it seems, is subject to the overriding judgment of the jury: '... gross negligence which the jury consider justifies criminal conviction ...'

(3) RECKLESS MANSLAUGHTER

R v Lidar [2004] held that *Adomako* had not abolished subjective reckless manslaughter. This applies where the defendant commits the *actus reus* of murder, foresaw a risk that the victim would suffer serious injury or death and took that risk.

There are other forms of homicide that are outside the scope of this chapter. These include offences by organisations under the Corporate Manslaughter and Corporate Homicide Act 2007 and offences specific to motorists (such as causing death by dangerous driving and causing death by careless or inconsiderate driving under the Road Traffic Act 1988).

REFORM

The Law Commission (2006) advocated comprehensive reform of the law on homicide which proposed that the offence of murder ought to be divided into first degree and second degree murder. First degree murder would be charged only where the defendant intended to kill or intended to do serious injury with an awareness of a risk of causing death. Second degree murder would be charged where the defendant intended to cause serious injury or intended to cause some injury with an awareness of a risk of causing death.

Second degree murder would also subsume voluntary manslaughter. Provocation, diminished responsibility and suicide pacts would remain partial defences.

Manslaughter would be retained as the equivalent to involuntary manslaughter. Killing through gross negligence, killing through a criminal act intended to cause injury or killing through a criminal act which the defendant was aware involved the risk of injury would fall into this category.

SUMMARY

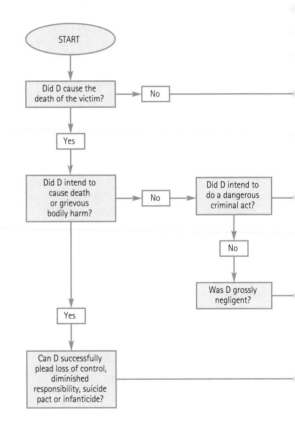

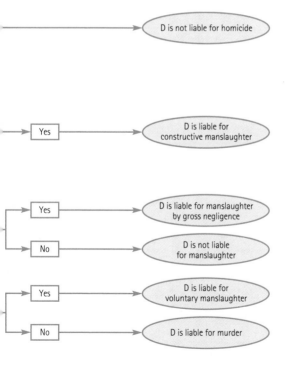

D is not liable for homicide

Yes → D is liable for constructive manslaughter

Yes → D is liable for manslaughter by gross negligence

No → D is not liable for manslaughter

Yes → D is liable for voluntary manslaughter

No → D is liable for murder

You should now be confident that you would be able to tick all of the boxes on the checklist at the beginning of this chapter. To check your knowledge of Fatal offences why not visit the companion website and take the Multiple Choice Question test. Check your understanding of the terms and vocabulary used in this chapter with the flashcard glossary.

Offences against property

Theft

Robbery

Burglary

Criminal damage

Fraud

Making off without payment

Handling stolen goods

This chapter concludes our analysis of particular offences by examining offences against property.

(1) THEFT

Definition

The basic definition of theft is to be found in s 1(1) of the Theft Act 1968, which provides that a person who:

> ... dishonestly appropriates property belonging to another with the intention of permanently depriving the other of it

is guilty of theft.

Relevant sections of Theft Act 1968

Dishonestly	appropriates	property	belonging to another	with the intention of permanently depriving the other of it
s 2	s 3	s 4	s 5	s 6

Actus reus

The *actus reus* of the offence is 'appropriating property belonging to another'.

Appropriation

Appropriation is defined in s 3(1) of the Theft Act 1968 as

any assumption by a person or the rights of an owner.

The phrase 'any *assumption* by a person of the rights of an owner' means that the thief has taken to himself rights which he does not have and is dealing with the property as if he was the legal owner.

The term 'the rights of the owner' includes not only the owner's right to owner-ship but also other rights he may have. It includes rights to possession or control, the right to use the property, to sell it, to give it away and so on.

Appropriation can, therefore, take many forms, including:

- offering the property for sale (*R v Pitham and Hehl* [1976]);
- taking the property;
- pledging the property;
- destroying the property;
- fixing the price of the property (*R v Morris* [1983]).

In *R v Gomez* [1993], the House of Lords decided that any interference with property belonging to another would amount to an appropriation, irrespective of whether the owner consented or authorised the act in question.

> ### ▶ R v GOMEZ [1993]
>
> **Property can be appropriated with or without the owner's consent and only one right of the owner need be assumed.**
>
> Facts
>
> The defendant was charged with theft after wittingly deceiving his manager into believing cheques given for goods from a rogue were good.

91

> **Held**
>
> It was irrelevant that the owner had consented to the goods changing ownership, any interference with property belonging to another would amount to appropriation. Obviously for the offence of theft to be complete the relevant *mens rea* is also required.

As *Gomez* was a case where, on the facts, consent was obtained by fraud, it was thought that its *ratio* could be restricted to such cases. However, in *R v Hinks* [2000], the House of Lords held that the defendant could be guilty of theft even though the property had been validly transferred to her in the form of a gift. The House of Lords rejected arguments that the word 'appropriate' should be interpreted as if the word 'unlawfully' preceded it. The result is that everything depends on the defendant's state of mind, in particular whether or not the defendant is dishonest.

Property

Section 4(1) of the Theft Act 1968 defines 'property' as:

> ... money and all other property, real or personal, including things in action and other intangible property.

This seemingly all-encompassing definition is subject to both common law and statutory exceptions. The following do not constitute property:

- information (*Oxford v Moss* [1979]);

- electricity (*Low v Blease* [1975]);

- a human corpse (*R v Sharpe* [1857]);

- land (s 4(2));

- wild plants (s 4(3));

- wild animals (s 4(4)).

However, there are also some exceptions to the exceptions, rendering some of the above capable of being stolen in certain circumstances:

- a human corpse does become property capable of being stolen if skill or effort has been exercised on it (*Doodeward v Spence* [1907]); moreover, products of the body, such as blood and urine, are capable of being stolen (*R v Rothery* [1976]; *R v Welsh* [1974]). In *R v Kelly* [1998], the Court of Appeal held that human body parts are capable of being the subject of a charge of theft if they have acquired different attributes by virtue of the application of skill, such as dissection or preservation techniques;

- land can be appropriated by (a) a trustee, personal representative or liquidator; (b) someone not in possession can appropriate anything severed from the land; and (c) a tenant can appropriate any fixture (s 4(2)(a), (b) and (c));

- wild plants can be stolen if the whole plant is taken or the plant is taken for sale or reward (s 4(3));

- wild animals can be stolen if they are tamed or ordinarily kept in captivity or have been, or are in the process of being, reduced into another's possession (s 4(4)).

Belonging to another

The basic definition of 'belonging to another' is contained in s 5(1) of the Theft Act 1968:

> Property shall be regarded as belonging to any person having possession or control of it, or having in it any proprietary right or interest . . .

Property will 'belong to another' if someone else possesses, controls or has a proprietary right or interest in the property. Whilst possession requires some degree of knowledge (*Warner v MPC* [1969]), control does not (*R v Woodman* [1974]).

In *Ricketts v Basildon Magistrates' Court* [2010], it was held that items left outside charity shops could be regarded as property belonging to another. However, until the charity shop took possession of the item, the other to whom the property belonged was the person who had donated the item.

A proprietary right or interest would include equitable interests. Property may therefore 'belong to another' even if the defendant owns it.

Thus, in *R v Turner No 2* [1971], an owner was convicted of theft of his car when he removed it from a garage where it was undergoing repairs without informing the proprietor. Since the garage had possession and control, the car was treated as if it belonged to another in accordance with s 5(1).

Section 5(3) of the Theft Act 1968 extends the meaning of 'belonging to another':

> Where a person receives property from or on account of another, and is under an obligation to the other to retain and deal with that property or its proceeds in a particular way, the property or proceeds shall be regarded (as against him) as belonging to another.

As the 'obligation' must be legally enforceable (*R v Gilks* [1972]), this will normally involve either contractual obligations or obligations imposed under a statute.

The terms of the contractual or statutory duty must be examined in order to establish the precise nature of the obligation. If the defendant is permitted to do what he likes with the property, his only obligation being to account in due course for an equivalent sum, s 5(3) does not apply (*R v Hall* [1973]). However, the defendant need not be under an obligation to retain particular monies; it is sufficient that he is under an obligation to keep in existence a fund equivalent to that which he has received (*Lewis v Lethbridge* [1987]).

It would appear that s 5(3) will apply where someone contracts on the basis that the money he hands over will be transferred by the recipient to a stakeholder or trustee. The recipient is under an obligation to deal with the money in a particular way and, if he dishonestly appropriates it, can be convicted of theft (*R v Kineberg and Marsden* [1998]).

Section 5(4) covers the situation where the defendant receives property by mistake:

> Where a person gets property by another's mistake, and is under an obligation to make restitution ... then ... the property or proceeds shall be regarded (as against him) as belonging to the person entitled to restoration.

This could cover the following possible situations:

- mistaken overpayment of wages (*AG's Reference (No 1 of 1983)* [1984]);
- mistaken crediting of a bank account (*R v Shadrokh-Cigari* [1988]).

In addition, it is thought that the sub-section would apply to situations where the defendant receives too much change or too many goods by mistake.

Mens rea

The *mens rea* required is twofold. First it must be proved that the defendant acted dishonestly. Second, it must be proved that the defendant acted with the intention to permanently deprive the other.

Dishonesty

There is a negative definition of dishonesty set out in s 2(1) of the Theft Act 1968. A person is not dishonest if he appropriates in the honest belief that:

- he has a legal right to deprive another of the property (s 2(1)(a));

- he would have the other's consent if the other knew of the appropriation and the circumstances of it (s 2(1)(b));

- the person to whom the property belongs cannot be discovered by taking reasonable steps (s 2(1)(c)).

The Act also states that a person may be dishonest even though they are willing to pay for the property (s 2(2)) and that it matters not whether the defendant appropriated the property to make a gain or whether there is any benefit to the thief (s 1(2)).

So, the Act does not actually provide a definition of dishonesty. Instead it is a question of fact for the jury. A positive test for establishing dishonesty was laid down by the Court of Appeal in *R v Ghosh* [1982]. In cases of doubt, the jury should be given the following direction:

> Was the defendant dishonest according to the standards of ordinary decent people? If yes, did the defendant realise that what he was doing was dishonest by these standards?

The first purely objective limb of the Ghosh test has been criticised as assuming that there exists a clear set of moral standards that the jury can apply. In reality, the jury will be applying their morality. A defendant will be found to be dishonest according to the first test if they are more immoral than their jurors.

Note that this test does not require the defendant himself to consider what he has done to be dishonest. The second limb of the test is whether he realised what he was doing was dishonest by those objective standards.

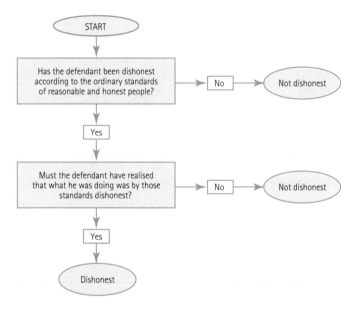

Intention to permanently deprive

The Theft Act 1968 preserved the rule at common law and under the Larceny Act 1916 that appropriating property of another with the intention to deprive them only temporally of it is not stealing.

However, s 6 provides that the needed intention will be met if the defendant has the intention 'to treat the thing as his own to dispose of'.

Section 6(1) provides that an intention to borrow or lend of a property may suffice if the borrowing or lending is 'for a period and in such circumstances equivalent to an outright taking'.

In relation to s 6(1), the intention to permanently deprive will be deemed to exist if the defendant intended to return the goods in a fundamentally changed state so that virtually all of their value would have been lost (*R v Lloyd* [1985]). Similarly, someone who deals with property knowing that he is doing so in a way which risks its loss may be intending to 'treat the thing as his own to dispose of regardless of the other's rights' and may, therefore, be deemed to have an intention to permanently deprive under s 6(1) (*R v Fernandes* [1995]).

In *R v Marshall, Coombes and Eren* [1998], it was held that someone who buys an Underground ticket from a passenger and sells it on could be guilty of theft by virtue of s 6(1).

In *Marshall* the Court of Appeal held that the tickets still belonged to the railway company because there was a term to that extent on the reverse of the ticket. The decision is controversial, however, since it is unclear whether this would be definitive under the law of contract.

Section 6(2) provides that if the defendant pledges the property as security for a loan, then he will be deemed to have intended to deprive the victim of the property permanently. This covers unauthorised pawning.

The problem of 'joy-riding' is dealt with specifically under the Theft Act 1968. Section 12 provides a specific offence of taking a conveyance which does not require the defendant to intend to permanently deprive the other. 'Conveyance' refers to a car, a motorbike, a boat or anything else constructed or adapted for the carriage of a person or persons. Section 12A provides for a more serious form of this offence where there has been death, serious injury or damage to property other than the vehicle.

(2) ROBBERY

Definition

Section 8(1) of the Theft Act 1968 provides that:

> A person is guilty of robbery if he steals and immediately before or at the time of doing so, and in order to do so, he uses force on any person or puts or seeks to put any person in fear of being then and there subjected to force.

Actus reus

Force

As can be seen from the above definition, the Act requires proof of either the use or the threat of force against the person. Whether force actually has been used or threatened is a matter for the jury to decide (*R v Dawson* [1976]).

The force can be used or threatened against any person, not necessarily the owner of the property (*Smith v Desmond Hall* [1965]).

It is clear that the force or threat of force must occur before or at the time of stealing, and in order to steal. The use of force even seconds after the appropriation has taken place would not amount to robbery. However, the courts have been prepared on some occasions to hold that an appropriation could consist of a continuing act (*R v Hale* [1978]).

Stealing

All the elements required for s 1(1) theft are necessary to establish that the defendant has stolen for the purposes of robbery. Thus, in *R v Robinson* [1977], the defendant's conviction for robbery was quashed on the basis that, since he honestly believed that he was entitled to the property in question, he was not dishonest under s 2(1)(a) and, therefore, was incapable of committing theft.

Mens rea

The same *mens rea* as for theft (see earlier) is required but there must also be an intention to use force.

(3) BURGLARY

Definitions

Section 9 of the Theft Act 1968 creates two burglary offences.

Section 9(1)(a)

By s 9(1)(a), a person is guilty of burglary if 'he enters any building or part of a building as a trespasser' with an intention to:

- steal;

- inflict grievous bodily harm;

- commit unlawful damage to the building or anything therein.

Note that s 63 of the Sexual Offences Act 2003 introduces a new offence of *trespass with intent to commit a sexual offence*, which replaces and expands on the old offence of entering as a trespasser with intent to rape (previously charged under s 9(1)(a)).

Section 9(1)(b)

A person is guilty of this offence if, having entered a building or part of a building as a trespasser, he steals or attempts to steal or inflict grievous bodily harm.

Actus reus

Both burglary offences require that the defendant has entered a building or part of a building as a trespasser.

Building or part of a building

In the Act there is no complete definition of what constitutes a 'building'. The following points should be noted in this respect:

▓ inhabited vehicles or vessels will amount to a 'building' for the purposes of the Act, even when the inhabiting person is not there;

▓ in *Stevens v Gourley* [1859], it was stated that a building was 'a structure of considerable size and intended to be permanent or at least to endure for a considerable length of time';

▓ in *B and S v Leathley* [1979], a large freezer container without wheels and which was connected to the electricity supply was held to constitute a building;

▓ in *Norfolk Constabulary v Seekings and Gould* [1986], a lorry trailer with wheels, used for storage and connected to the electricity supply, was held not to be a building;

▓ in *R v Walkington* [1979], a customer who went behind a till counter was held to enter part of a building as a trespasser.

Entry

Section 9 requires that the defendant must enter, or have entered, a building or part of a building. In *R v Collins* [1972], it was held that an entry must be 'effective and substantial'.

In *R v Brown* [1985], a case which involved the defendant leaning through a broken shop window, it was held that the crucial word in the *Collins* test was 'effective' and that 'substantial' did not materially assist in the matter. As the defendant was able to reach the articles he wished to steal, his entry was held to be 'effective' and the conviction was upheld.

Similarly, in *R v Ryan* [1995], a defendant who had his head and arm trapped inside a building by a window was held to have entered for the purposes of burglary. In the light of *Brown* and *Ryan*, it seems that the courts are adopting a very broad approach to the 'effective' and/or 'substantial' test established in *Collins*.

As a trespasser

The defendant must not only enter a building, he must do so as a trespasser. A trespasser is someone who enters property without express or implied permission.

A defendant who has permission to enter for particular purposes, but then exceeds the express or implied conditions of entry, will enter as a trespasser. For example, in *R v Smith and Jones* [1976], the defendants had permission to enter the house of Smith's father for normal domestic purposes, but not in order to steal the television set.

Mens rea

The *mens rea* required is that the defendant must enter as a trespasser with intention or being reckless as to whether he is a trespasser (*R v Collins* [1972]).

(4) CRIMINAL DAMAGE

Definitions

Section 1(1) Criminal Damage Act 1971

This sub-section provides that the 'basic' offence of criminal damage is committed where:

A person who without lawful excuse destroys or damages any property belonging to another, intending to destroy or damage any such property or being reckless as to whether any such property would be destroyed or damaged.

Section 1(2)

This sub-section states that an 'aggravated' offence is committed where:

A person who without lawful excuse destroys or damages any property, whether belonging to himself or another:

(a) intending to destroy or damage any property or being reckless as to whether any property would be destroyed or damaged; and

(b) intending by the destruction or damage to endanger the life of another or being reckless as to whether the life of another would be thereby endangered.

Section 1(3)

This sub-section provides that where property is destroyed or damaged by fire, the offence is charged as arson and is punishable with a maximum sentence of life imprisonment.

Actus reus

Property

Property is defined in s 10(1) as anything of 'a tangible nature, whether real or personal, including money'.

Although somewhat similar to the definition of 'property' provided in s 4 of the Theft Act 1968, it should be noted that criminal damage can be committed in relation to land: while land cannot be stolen, conversely, intangible property can be stolen, but cannot be the subject of criminal damage.

Belonging to another

The property must belong to another for the purposes of s 1(1), but need not belong to another in relation to the s 1(2) offence.

Property will be treated as 'belonging to another' for the purposes of s 1(1) if that other has custody or control of it or has any proprietary right or interest in it or has a charge on it (s 10(2)).

Damage

Whether property has been destroyed or damaged will depend upon the circumstances of each case, the nature of the article and the way in which it is affected. The following cases provide illustrations of acts which were held to have amounted to criminal damage:

■ in *Blake v DPP* [1993], a biblical quotation written on a concrete pillar with a marker pen was held to amount to criminal damage;

■ similarly, in *Hardman and Others v Chief Constable of Avon and Somerset Constabulary* [1986], the spraying of human silhouettes by CND supporters on pavements was held to constitute criminal damage notwithstanding that the figures would be washed away by the next rainfall;

■ in *Roe v Kingerlee* [1986], it was held that the application of mud to the walls of a cell could amount to damage as it would cost money to remove it;

■ in *R v Henderson and Battley* [1984] the unauthorised dumping of waste on a building site which cost £2,000 to remove was held to constitute criminal damage;

■ in *Samuel v Stubbs* [1972], criminal damage was held to have been done to a policeman's helmet when it had been jumped upon causing a 'temporary functional derangement'.

The following two cases illustrate actions which were not held to have amounted to criminal damage:

■ in *A (A Juvenile) v R* [1978], a football supporter who spat on a policeman's coat was found not to have committed criminal damage since the coat did not require cleaning or other expenditure;

■ in *Morphitis v Salmon* [1990] a scratch caused to a scaffolding bar did not amount to criminal damage since its value or usefulness was not impaired.

Mens rea

The 'basic' section 1(1) offence

The *mens rea* required for the basic offence of criminal damage is an intention to do an act which would cause damage to property belonging to another or being reckless in relation to such an act.

In *R v G* [2004] recklessness for the purposes of the 1971 Act was defined as follows:

A person acts recklessly within the meaning of section 1 of the Criminal Damage Act 1971 with respect to:
(i) a circumstance when he is aware of a risk that it exists or will exist;
(ii) a result when he is aware of a risk that it will occur;

and it is, in the circumstances known to him, unreasonable to take the risk.

As explained in Chapter 1, the previous definition of recklessness propounded by the majority in *R v Caldwell* [1982] is no longer good law.

The 'aggravated' section 1(2) offence

The *mens rea* for this more serious form of criminal damage consists of an intention to damage property and an intention that the damaged property endangers life, or recklessness as to whether this occurs.

There is no need for life to actually be endangered. All that is required is that the defendant intended the damage to endanger life, or was reckless as to whether this occurred (*R v Dudley* [1989]).

However, the defendant's *mens rea* as to whether life is endangered must extend to the consequences of the criminal damage and not be limited merely to the act causing the damage. For example, in *R v Steer* [1980], the defendant's conviction under s 1(2) for firing rifle shots at the windows of his victim's house was quashed on appeal. There was no evidence that he intended or was reckless as to whether the broken glass, as opposed to the shots themselves, would endanger life.

Defences

Honest belief in the owner's consent is a defence under s 5(2)(a), which provides that a person will have a lawful excuse if:

... he believed that the person or persons whom he believed to be entitled to consent to the destruction of or damage to the property in question has so consented, or would have so consented to it if he or they had known of the destruction or damage and its circumstances.

Defence of property

Under s 5(2)(b), the defendant will have a lawful excuse if, in order to protect property, he damaged other property provided he believed that the property was in immediate need of protection and that the means of protection were reasonable in the circumstances.

Section 5(3) clearly provides that the defendant's belief that his actions are reasonable does not itself have to be reasonable. However, the courts have sometimes appeared reluctant to judge defendants on the basis of what they considered to be reasonable in the circumstances (see *Blake v DPP* [1993]).

(5) FRAUD

Prior to the Fraud Act 2006 the offences involving deception were very technical and covered two Theft Acts. The law was particularly complex. These offences have now been abolished by s 1 Fraud Act 2006.

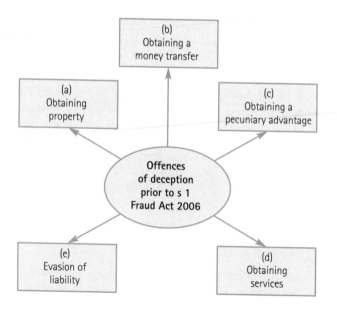

Under the old law, it was necessary to prove that:

1 the defendant deceived someone;

2 that deception caused the defendant to obtain the relevant thing;

3 the defendant acted dishonestly (applying the *Ghosh* test);

4 the defendant actually obtained the relevant thing (property, money transfer, pecuniary advantage, service or evasion of liability).

The relevant thing would determine which offence the defendant was charged with.

The Fraud Act 2006

Now the offences of deception have been abolished there is only one offence of fraud (see s 1 Fraud Act 2006). This offence can be committed in three ways under ss 2–4. Fraud can be committed by false representation (s 2), by failing to disclose information (s 3) or by abuse of position (s 4).

It is not necessary for there to be an actual gain or loss. However, there must be an intention to make an economic gain or loss (s 5). The new law is different to the old law in two main respects. First, deception has been removed. Second, there is now no need for the defendant to actually obtain anything. Both of these changes were made so that online fraud was covered by the new law.

Fraud by false representation

Section 2 provides:

A fraud is committed by way of false representation under s 2 where D:

(a) dishonestly makes a false representation, and

(b) intends, by making the representation:

   (i) to make a gain for himself or another, or

   (ii) to cause loss to another or to expose another to a risk of loss.

Actus reus

The offence will be committed when a defendant makes either an express or implied false representation as to either fact or law. It is not necessary for there to be an actual gain or loss.

Mens rea

The defendant must know the representation is false or know it might be false or misleading. The representation must be made dishonestly (*Ghosh* applies) and the defendant must make the representation intending to make a gain for themselves or cause a loss or a risk of loss to the victim.

The Act makes it clear that fraud can be committed where a person makes a representation to a machine. Moreover, the Act only covers economic crimes. The intended 'gain or loss' must be 'in money or other property'.

Fraud by failing to disclose information

Section 3 creates the offence of fraud by failing to disclose information. It provides that a person commits this offence when a person:

(a) dishonestly fails to disclose to another person information which he is under a legal duty to disclose, and

(b) intends, by failing to disclose the information:

  (i) to make a gain for himself or another, or

  (ii) to cause loss to another or to expose another to a risk of loss.

Actus reus

The offence is committed where the defendant fails to disclose information which they are under a 'legal duty to disclose'. A legal duty to disclose information may be imposed by contract (oral or written), by statute, or from the existence of a fiduciary relationship.

Mens rea

The failure to disclose must be dishonestly made and the defendant must intend to make a gain or cause a loss.

Fraud by abuse of a position of trust

Section 4 creates the offence of fraud by abuse of position which would cover trustees, bankers, solicitors for example. It is committed where a person:

(a) occupies a position in which he is expected to safeguard, or not to act against, the financial interests of another person,

(b) dishonestly abuses that position, and

(c) intends, by means of the abuse of that position:

    (i) to make a gain for himself or another, or

    (ii) to cause loss to another or to expose another to a risk of loss.

A person may be regarded as having abused his position even though his conduct consisted of an omission rather than an act.

Actus reus

The *actus reus* is twofold: the defendant must occupy a relevant position and there must be an abuse of that position. The term 'abuse of that position' is not limited by a definition, because it is intended to cover a wide range of conduct. It will apply, for example, in the context of trustee and beneficiary, director and client, principal and agent, employee and employer.

Mens rea

The abuse of position must be dishonest and the defendant must intend to make a gain or cause a loss.

Dishonestly obtaining services

The offence of obtaining services by deception under s 1(1) of the Theft Act 1978 has also been replaced with a new offence. Section 11 of the Fraud Act 2006 creates the offence of dishonestly obtaining services. This is a result crime and no deception or false representation is required. It is limited to defendants who intend to avoid payment or payment in full.

Actus reus

The offence is committed where the defendant obtains, by an act, chargeable services without having paid for them.

Mens rea

The *mens rea* is threefold:

1 the defendant's act must be done dishonestly;

2 the defendant must know that payment is, or may be, expected;

3 the defendant must have the intention that payment will not be made (or not made in full).

The needed intention may be implied from the defendant's conduct. In *DPP v Ray* [1974] students ordered a meal intending to pay but then changed their minds, running off without paying. The House of Lords held that the whole scenario should be seen as a continuing act. By sitting in the restaurant, the students originally made a true representation that they would pay. This became a false representation once they had changed their mind but maintained the demeanour of ordinary customers.

(6) MAKING OFF WITHOUT PAYMENT

Definition
Section 3(1) of the Theft Act 1978 provides:

> ... a person who, knowing that payment on the spot for any goods supplied or service done is required or expected from him, dishonestly makes off without having paid as required or expected and with intent to avoid payment of the amount due shall be guilty of an offence.

Actus reus
The offence will not be committed if the payment is not legally enforceable or where the supply of goods or the doing of the service is contrary to law (s 3(3)).

It seems that, for the offence to be complete, the defendant must have 'made off' by leaving the premises where payment is due (*R v McDavitt* [1981]).

Failing to pay includes leaving an inadequate amount, counterfeit notes or foreign currency. It would also include using another's cheque or credit card or leaving a cheque that will be dishonoured. No liability under s 3 arises where the defendant induces the victim to waive the right to payment by exercising a deception (*R v Vincent* [2001]).

Mens rea
The defendant must know that payment on the spot is required and intend to permanently avoid payment and to be dishonest.

In *R v Allen* [1985], the House of Lords held that an intention to temporarily avoid payment would not suffice. The defendant incurred a hotel bill and left without paying intending to pay later after some business transactions. The Court of Appeal and the House of Lords quashed his conviction. He had not intended to avoid payment permanently.

> **R v McDAVITT [1981]**

Making off without payment actually requires the defendant to leave the premises where the payment is due.

Facts

Following an argument about his bill, the defendant hid in the toilet waiting for the police.

Held

The Court of Appeal held that making off meant making off from the spot where payment is required or expected. In this case the spot was the restaurant. The jury should have been directed that they could not convict of this offence but it was open to them to convict of attempting to make off without payment.

(7) HANDLING STOLEN GOODS

Definitions

Section 22 of the Theft Act 1968 provides:

> A person handles stolen goods if (otherwise than in the course of stealing) knowing or believing them to be stolen goods he dishonestly receives the goods, or dishonestly undertakes or assists in their retention, removal, disposal or realisation by or for the benefit of another.

Some of the key terms used in this section are themselves subject to further statutory definition. For example, s 34(2)(b) states that 'goods' include:

> money and every other description of property except land and includes things severed from the land by stealing.

From this definition, it would appear that choses in action, such as a bank account into which money obtained in exchange for stolen property has been paid, will constitute stolen goods (*R v Pritchley* [1973]; *AG's Reference (No 4 of 1979)* [1980]).

In addition, s 24(4) makes it clear that, in order to constitute stolen property, the goods must have been obtained as a result of theft, obtaining property by deception or blackmail.

However, goods will lose their 'stolen' status if they are restored to the person from whom they were stolen or to other lawful possession or custody (s 24(3)). Thus, in *Haughton v Smith* [1975], tins of meat ceased to be 'stolen' when police took control of the lorry transporting them.

What constitutes 'custody' seems to depend on the degree of control exercised over the goods. For example, in *AG's Reference (No 1 of 1974)* [1974], the Court of Appeal was unwilling to hold that a police officer who immobilised a car, which he suspected of containing stolen goods, by removing its rotor arm had taken custody of the property.

In a situation where goods have ceased to be 'stolen' because they have been taken into lawful custody, a defendant who handles them in the belief that they are stolen could be liable for attempting to handle stolen goods contrary to s 1(1) of the Criminal Attempts Act 1981.

It should be noted that, where stolen goods have been exchanged for other forms of property, that other property may also constitute 'stolen goods'. Section 24(2) provides that, for goods to be stolen, they must be, or have been, in the hands of the thief or handler and directly or indirectly represent the stolen goods in whole or in part.

Actus reus

Modes of handling

Mode	Action	Benefits another	Omission
Receiving	Taking into possession or control	Not necessary	Action required
Removal	Movement of goods	For another's benefit	Action required
Realisation	Sale or exchange of goods	For another's benefit	Action required
Disposal	Destroying or hiding	For another's benefit	Action required
Retention	Keeping not losing	For another's benefit	Possible by omission
NB: Arranging to do any of the above in itself is an offence			

■ *Receiving*

Taking possession of the stolen property. It is not necessary to show that the defendant acted 'for the benefit of another'.

■ *Removal*

Moving the stolen goods from one place to another. The transportation must be for 'the benefit of another'.

■ *Realisation*

Selling or exchanging the stolen goods. The realisation must be 'for the benefit of another'.

■ *Disposal*

Destroying or hiding the stolen goods. The disposal must be 'for the benefit of another'.

■ *Retention*

Keeping possession of the stolen goods. The retention must be 'for the benefit of another'. It seems that a mere omission to inform the police of the presence of stolen property will not amount to retention (*R v Brown* [1970]). However, in *R v Kanwar* [1982], a defendant who deliberately misled the police as to the presence of stolen goods in her home was held to have assisted her husband in their retention.

As well as the above five modes of handling, it is also an offence to arrange to do any of these things or to assist in the removal, realisation, disposal or retention of stolen goods by another person (s 22(1)).

For the benefit of another

All the above modes of handling, with the exception of receiving and arranging to receive, require that the defendant act 'for the benefit of another'. It follows that a defendant who knowingly sells stolen goods for his own benefit will not be liable for arranging, assisting or undertaking the realisation of stolen property. The innocent purchaser would not be 'another person' within the meaning of the sub-section (*R v Bloxham* [1983]).

Otherwise than in the course of stealing

The above words, included in the definition of the offence, are necessary to prevent many instances of theft from automatically becoming handling as well. Despite the decision of the Court of Appeal in *R v Pitham and Hehl* [1977], it would seem that the phrase 'course of stealing' clearly implies a continuous rather than an instantaneous act. However, such a continuous act concept entails obvious uncertainties about precisely when the act commences and terminates. The practical solution is to allow the jury to decide this matter on a case by case basis.

Mens rea

There are two elements to the *mens rea* of handling: dishonesty and knowledge or belief that the goods are stolen.

In relation to dishonesty, the *Ghosh* test can be applied in cases of difficulty, but should not be automatically resorted to (*R v Roberts* [1987]).

A belief that the property is stolen is a purely subjective matter and should not be equated with what the reasonable person would have believed in the same circumstances (*Atwal v Massey* [1971]).

Where there is evidence that should have made the defendant suspect that the goods were stolen, the jury are entitled to infer a belief that they were stolen (*R v Lincoln* [1980]). However, mere suspicion is not to be equated with such a belief (*R v Grainge* [1974]).

In the absence of a satisfactory explanation to the contrary, a jury is entitled to infer a belief that the property is stolen where there is evidence that the defendant came into possession of the goods soon after the theft.

You should now be confident that you would be able to tick all of the boxes on the checklist at the beginning of this chapter. To check your knowledge of Offences against property why not visit the companion website and take the Multiple Choice Question test. Check your understanding of the terms and vocabulary used in this chapter with the flashcard glossary.

General defences

Insanity

Automatism

Age

Intoxication

Necessity

Duress

Self-defence

Mistake

As a general principle, a person is only found liable of a criminal offence if they have committed the *actus reus* of the crime, with the needed *mens rea* and if they cannot rely upon a defence. This chapter explores general defences which defendants may seek to rely on. It overlaps with all of the previous chapters. For instance, if you are answering a problem question on sexual offences, the facts of the problem may well require you to discuss whether the defendant could rely on one or more of the defences which are explained here.

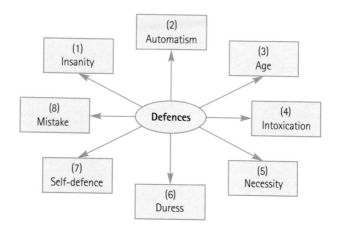

(1) INSANITY

Where the defendant claims to have been suffering at the time of the offence from some sort of mental disturbance or impairment, then automatism, insanity and, in murder cases, diminished responsibility may all be considered. Diminished responsibility was considered above, under 'Homicide'.

The major difference between insanity and automatism is that whilst insanity results from an internal cause, automatism results from an external cause.

It should be noted that insanity, unlike automatism, will not provide a defence to crimes of strict liability (*DPP v H* [1997]).

Defence	Nature	When relevant	Effect of successful plea
Automatism	Body acts without control of the mind.	At the time of the offence	Not guilty
Insanity	Disease of the mind which renders the defendant incapable of knowing:	At the time of the offence	Not guilty by reason of insanity
Insanity	Disease of the mind which renders the defendant incapable of knowing: (a) the nature and quality of his actions; or (b) that his actions are legally wrong.	At the time of the offence	Not guilty by reason of insanity

Insanity may be raised by the prosecution, the defendant or the judge. The judge may raise the defence and leave it to the jury if he concludes that the evidence supports such a defence.

If the defendant raised the defence, he bears the burden of proving it. This is an exception to the general rule that it is the prosecution to prove the guilt of the defendant beyond reasonable doubt and to disprove any defence he may raise. If the defendant raises the defence, the lower civil standard of proof applies: he must prove it on the balance of probabilities.

Where the defendant is found to be insane, the prosecution needs only to prove beyond reasonable doubt that the defendant committed the *actus reus* of the crime. The special verdict requires no proof of any *mens rea* for the crime with which the defendant is charged.

Previously, being found 'not guilty by reason of insanity' mandated a judge to order detention for life under s 2 of the Trial of Lunatics Act 1883. However, this is no longer the only possible result. Since 1991, a judge may make a treatment or supervision order or grant an absolute discharge (Criminal Procedure (Insanity and Unfitness to Plead) Act 1991).

Definition
In 1843, Daniel M'Naghten, intending to murder Sir Robert Peel, killed his secretary by mistake. Following his acquittal on grounds of insanity, the judges

formulated the so called *M'Naghten* rules which have since become accepted as providing a comprehensive definition of insanity (*R v Sullivan* [1984]).

According to these rules, it must be proved (by the defence, on a balance of probabilities) that, at the time the offence was committed, the defendant was labouring under such a defect of reason, arising from a disease of the mind, so as not to know the nature and quality of the act he was doing, or, if he did know it, that he did not know that what he was doing was wrong.

The nature and quality of the act

As we have noted, one of the two grounds for establishing insanity under the *M'Naghten* rules is that the defendant's disease of the mind prevented him from being aware of his actions. For example, in *R v Kemp* [1957], the defendant was found not guilty by reason of insanity when he was unaware of his actions during a 'blackout' caused by a disease of the body which affected the mind.

Did not know that the action was wrong

The second ground for establishing the defence is that, because of a disease of the mind, the defendant did not know that his actions were wrong. 'Wrong', in this context, has been interpreted to mean legally, as opposed to morally, wrong (*R v Windle* [1952]).

Disease of the mind

Although medical evidence will be of relevance, whether a particular condition amounts to a disease of the mind is a legal, not a medical question.

It seems that any disease which affects the functioning of the mind is a disease of the mind. Examples would include epilepsy, diabetes, arteriosclerosis and even sleepwalking (*R v Hennessy* [1989]; *R v Kemp* [1957]; *R v Burgess* [1991]).

A disease is something *internal* to the defendant, therefore: 'A malfunctioning of the mind of transitory effect caused by the application to the body of some external factor such as violence, drugs, including anaesthetics, alcohol and hypnotic influences cannot fairly be said to be due to disease' (*per* Lawton LJ in *R v Quick* [1973]).

An external cause might form the basis of a plea of non-insane automatism, provided it resulted in a total loss of control of the mind over the body.

A distinction may thus be drawn between internal and external factors. In relation to diabetes, for example: Hypoglycaemia, which is caused by failing to eat after taking insulin – is an external cause and **not** a disease of the mind (*R v Quick* [1973]) while hyperglycaemia, which is caused by failing to take insulin, is an internal cause and therefore is a disease of the mind (*R v Hennesey* [1989]).

Insanity: **The Three Steps**	[1] A defect of reason ...
	[2] Arising from a disease of the mind (that is, an internal cause) ...
	[3] Which means that the defendant did not know the nature and quality of the act he was doing or, if he did know, he did not know that what he was doing was (legally) wrong

(2) AUTOMATISM

Like the defence of insanity, this defence rests upon the idea that the defendant did not know what they were doing because the act was involuntary: the claim is that the defendant is not at fault because they were not a voluntary actor.

Automatism is a complete defence. The burden of disproving it is on the prosecution. The defence applies where the involuntariness is caused by an external cause and where there is a total loss of voluntary control.

The nature and quality of the act

The defence of automatism is limited to where the factor is external. A plea of automatism may be made, for example, if the defendant's muscles acted without his control of the mind as a reflex action of spasm (*Bratty v AG for Northern Ireland* [1963]).

Where cases include both external and internal factors both insanity and automatism may be left to the jury (*R v Roach* [2001]).

Total loss of control

The loss of control must be total. In *AG's Reference (No 2 of 1991)* [1993], a driver under a psychiatric condition drove on the hard shoulder but his body continued to control the vehicle. He was denied the defence of automatism. Although he was largely unaware of what was happening, his unawareness was not total.

117

Where the automatism is the defendant's fault

The defence covers the effect of prescribed drugs taken in accordance with medical advice.

If the defendant is at fault in bringing about the autonomic state, for example by voluntarily taking drugs, then he will have a defence to crimes of 'specific intent' but not those of 'basic intent' (*R v Lipman* [1970]; *R v Bailey* [1983]).

See '(4) Intoxication' for a discussion of the difference between crimes of specific and basic intent.

Automatism The Three Steps	[1] Involuntariness ...
	[2] Caused by an external cause ...
	[3] Which results in a total loss of control

(3) AGE

Rationale

The doctrine of *mens rea* is based on the presumption that criminal liability should only be imposed on those who are capable of understanding the nature and foreseeing the consequences of their actions. Exceptions are therefore made for children in the same way as they are made for adults whose actions are involuntary.

Children under 10 years of age

There is an *irrebuttable* presumption that a child under the age of 10 at the time of the alleged offence lacks the capacity to form the requisite *mens rea* (s 50 of the Children and Young Persons Act 1933). They are termed *doli incapax*.

Children between the ages of 10 and 14

Under s 34 of the Crime and Disorder Act 1998 children between 10 and 14 are not considered to be *doli incapax*. They are considered to be as responsible for their actions as adults. However, the defendant's young age will still be a factor in assessing the reasonableness of a defendant's actions where that is relevant (eg provocation) and also in assessing what was foreseen by the defendant in relation to crimes requiring intention or recklessness.

Children over 14 years of age

Children over 14 incur criminal liability on proof of *actus reus* and *mens rea* in the same way as adults.

Children and criminal liability

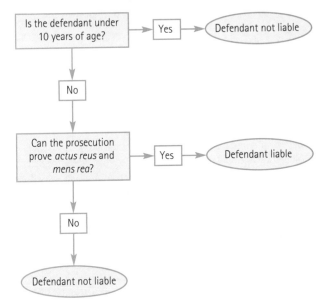

(4) INTOXICATION

Like the three other defences explored so far (insanity, automatism and age), intoxication is a capacity defence. It is a principle of criminal liability that a person should not be liable for their criminal actions if they were incapable of forming the needed *mens rea*. The claim here is that the defendant was incapable of forming the *mens rea* because he was intoxicated (through drink or drugs, lawful or unlawful).

The defendant's basic claim is that due to his intoxicated state, he did not form the *mens rea* required for the offence charged. If the defendant formed the necessary *mens rea*, then it is irrelevant that he was intoxicated at the time or that he has done something which he would not have done if sober.

Evidence of intoxication is always irrelevant to crimes of negligence and strict liability. In crimes of strict liability, the mental state of the defendant is irrelevant; in crimes of negligence, intoxication is irrelevant since the reasonable person is not intoxicated.

In relation to crimes requiring other forms of *mens rea*, the courts have distinguished involuntary intoxication from voluntary intoxication.

Involuntary intoxication

This is where the defendant does not know that he is taking an intoxicant. For example, the defendant's drink has been 'spiked'. Where the intoxication is involuntary the defendant will be entitled to a defence if the intoxication means that the defendant did not form the *mens rea* of the offence (*R v Kingston* [1994]).

If the defendant is mistaken as to the strength of the alcohol, this is voluntary intoxication (*R v Allen* [1988]). It should be noted that, where the defendant deliberately becomes intoxicated with the intention of giving himself confidence in order to commit an offence, the defence will not be allowed (*AG for Northern Ireland v Gallagher* [1963]).

Voluntary intoxication

This is where the intoxication is self-induced, the defendant knowingly consumes an intoxicant.

Where the intoxication is voluntary, intoxication is only relevant if the offence is one of 'specific intent' (*DDP v Beard* [1920]). If the crime is one of specific intent then intoxication is only a defence if it means that the defendant did not form the *mens rea* required.

Voluntary intoxication is always irrelevant in relation to crimes of basic intent.

The specific/basic distinction

Unfortunately, there is no clear overarching principle for distinguishing crimes of specific and basic intent. The term 'specific intent' was first coined by the then Lord Chancellor Lord Birkenhead in *DPP v Beard* [1920]. He recognised if the drunkenness had meant that the defendant did not form the needed *mens rea*, this would have been taken into account since 'specific intent is an essential element in the offence' of murder.

Later judgments gave the term 'specific intent' a specialised meaning which Lord Birkenhead probably never intended. Judges drew a distinction between crimes of specific and basic intent.

In *DDP v Majewski* [1977], the House of Lords held that intoxication was no defence since assault is an offence of basic intent. However, it is not clear from the judgments how the line between specific and basic intent is to be drawn.

View one: offences requiring evidence of intention are crimes of specific intent; offences requiring recklessness (or anything less than recklessness) are crimes of basic intent.

View two: only offences requiring ulterior intent (that is, further intent) are crimes of specific intent. A crime of further intent is an offence where the *mens rea* extends beyond the *actus reus*; if the *mens rea* and *actus reus* coincide, it is a crime of basic intent.

An example of a crime of ulterior intent is s 5(3) of the Misuse of Drugs Act 1971, which states that:

> it is an offence for a person to have a controlled drug in his possession, whether lawfully or not, with intent to supply it to another.

The *mens rea* here extends beyond the *actus reus*. The *actus reus* is fulfilled if the defendant has a controlled drug in his possession. The *mens rea* requires an intention that goes beyond possession: there must be an intention to supply.

Majewski is therefore authority for the proposition that evidence of voluntary intoxication negativing *mens rea* is only a defence to a charge of a crime requiring specific intent and not those requiring basic intent. Although this was enough to decide the case, Lord Elwyn Jones went further. His Lordship suggested that the condition of intoxication could constitute the culpability needed for any offence of basic intent. The 'prior fault' of the defendant in becoming intoxicated supplied the evidence of *mens rea* required.

Which of the two definitions of specific intent put forward in *Majewski* is to be preferred?

In *R v Caldwell* [1982], Lord Diplock expressed preference for the first view but this was mere *obiter*.

In *R v Heard* [2007] the Court of Appeal examined whether s 3 of the Sexual Offences Act 2003 is a crime of specific or basic intent. As described in Chapter 3, the *actus reus* of the offence is sexual touching without consent and the *mens rea* is that the touching is intentional and lack of reasonable belief as to consent. The Court of Appeal held that the offence was one of basic intent, despite the fact that the offence requires intention.

This seems to support the second view. The Court of Appeal held that the offence was one of basic intent since 'intentionally' in s 3 simply means deliberately rather than accidentally and did not show proof of an intention which goes beyond the prohibited act. In other words, it is not a crime of ulterior intent.

However, the Court of Appeal expressed doubt whether there was a simple test that could be applied to determine whether an offence is one of specific or basic intent. They seemed to place more emphasis on the fact that sexual offences were generally regarded as being offences of basic intent. The Court of Appeal deemed it unlikely that Parliament had intended to change the law by permitting reliance on voluntary intoxication where it previously had not been permitted. There was no basis for construing the Act as having altered the law.

However, the Court of Appeal recognised that it was of very limited help to try and label the offence as one particular type of intent because:

> There is . . . no universally logical test for distinguishing between crimes in which voluntary intoxication can be advanced as a defence and those in which it cannot; there is a large element of policy; categorisation is achieved on an offence by offence basis.

So ultimately the distinction rests upon the decisions of the courts. If the courts have previously dealt with the offence then their classification stands.

Note, however, that in relation to most crimes of specific intent, there will usually be an alternative offence of basic intent which the intoxicated defendant can be charged with instead. For example, instead of murder (a crime of specific intent), the defendant could be charged with manslaughter (a crime of basic intent).

The following lists provide some examples of offences that have been classified as crimes of specific and basic intent.

Crimes of specific intent

- Murder

- s 18 of the Offences Against the Person Act 1861

- s 24 of the Offences Against the Person Act 1861

- s 1(2) of the Criminal Damage Act 1971 (where the defendant intends to endanger life)

- ss 1, 8, 9, 21, 22, 25 of the Theft Act 1968

- s 1 of the Criminal Attempts Act 1981

- s 1 of the Criminal Law Act 1977

- Incitement

Crimes of basic intent

- Assault and battery

- ss 20, 23, 47 of the Offences Against the Person Act 1981

- Manslaughter

- Rape

- s 1(1) of the Criminal Damage Act 1971

- s 1(2) of the Criminal Damage Act 1971 (where the defendant is reckless as to whether life will be endangered)

Note that s 1(2) of the Criminal Damage Act 1971 is an offence of basic intent if the prosecution allege that it was committed recklessly and one of specific intent if they allege that it was committed intentionally.

The Law Commission (2009) has advocated codifying the existing common law on intoxication. The latest proposal differs from previous reports which favoured comprehensive legislation. It retains the substance of distinction between specific and basic intent but drops the terminology, providing instead a list of states of mind to which voluntary intoxication will be relevant.

General rule	Intoxication may be a defence to crimes of specific intent	Intoxication is not a defence to crimes of basic intent
Qualification	In all cases, intoxication only relevant if it means that defendant did not form the *mens rea* required. So, no defence if the mental element of the crime is negligence or strict liability or if the defendant has formed the *mens rea* anyway.	

	View One	View Two
Specific Intent =	Offences requiring evidence of intention are crimes of specific intent	Only offences requiring ulterior intent (that is, further intent) are crimes of specific intent
Basic Intent =	Offences requiring recklessness (or anything less than recklessness) are crimes of basic intent	All other offences are crimes of basic intent
Support for this distinction:	*R v Caldwell* [1982] But: mere *obiter*	*R v Heard* [2007] But: stressed no 'universally logical test'

Intoxication by 'dangerous drugs'

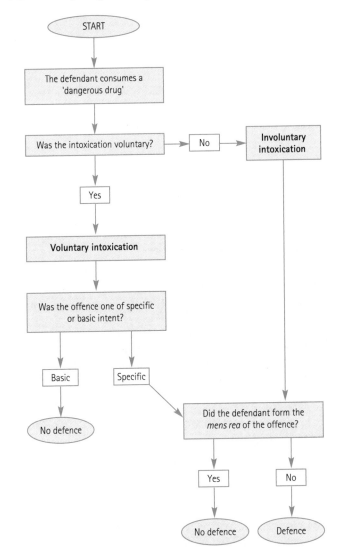

(5) NECESSITY

Rationale

The essence of the defence is that the defendant committed the crime in question in order to avoid an even greater evil. There are two reasons for recognising a defence of necessity in these circumstances:

- it is unjust to punish a defendant for doing something that a reasonable person would have done in the same circumstances; and

- the law should encourage a defendant to choose the lesser and avoid the greater evil on grounds of public policy.

Availability

Despite the above rationale, the courts have traditionally been somewhat reluctant to recognise a full blown defence of necessity. Indeed, in *R v Dudley and Stephens* [1884], Lord Coleridge CJ confirmed that necessity would not be available as a defence to theft of food and then went on to doubt whether it could ever be raised as a defence to homicide.

A distinction can be made between situations where the defendant claims to be acting out of necessity by killing the victim in order to preserve his own life, and the situation where the defendant kills A in order to save the life of B, the defendant not being under any threat of harm himself. In *Re A (Children) (Conjoined twins: surgical separation)* [2001], Brooke LJ stated that in such cases the defence of necessity would be available at common law to a doctor operating to separate conjoined twins, in the knowledge that to do so would cause the death of the weaker twin, provided:

- the defendant's act is needed to avoid inevitable and irreparable evil;

- no more should be done by the defendant than is reasonably necessary for the purpose to be achieved;

- the evil inflicted by the defendant's act must not be disproportionate to the evil avoided.

THE STATUTORY DEFENCE

The following statutory provisions contain what amounts to the defence of necessity, although it is not often explicitly referred to in this way:

- s 5(2)(b) of the Criminal Damage Act 1971;

- s 1(1) of the Infant Life (Preservation) Act 1929;

- s 1(4) of the Abortion Act 1967.

Necessity at common law

During the 1980s, in cases such as *R v Willer* [1986], *R v Conway* [1989] and *R v Martin* [1989], the courts showed a greater willingness to recognise the defence of necessity, initially in relation to road traffic offences, although there has been judicial recognition that the defence is not limited to such cases (*R v Pommell* [1995]).

On the basis of *Conway* and *Martin*, it would appear that, where there is some evidence of necessity, the matter should be left to the jury with the following direction:

- had the defendant felt compelled to act by what he perceived to be the grave danger of the situation? If so,

- would a sober person of reasonable firmness sharing the characteristics of the accused have responded to the perceived threat by acting as the accused had?

If the answers to both these questions are in the affirmative, the defence of necessity, always assuming it to be available, will be established.

(6) DURESS

Duress and necessity

The defences of duress and necessity are closely related. Indeed, the courts in cases such as *Conway* and *Martin* (above) did not explicitly refer to necessity, but to 'duress of circumstances', a phrase also adopted in the Draft Criminal Code Bill of 1989. Although both defences involve a situation where the defendant is faced with a choice of two evils, the major difference between them is the source of the evil. In relation to necessity, the defendant is forced by *circumstances* to break the law, whereas in duress the source of the evil is the threat of another person.

Definition

The defence of duress consists of a plea that the defendant felt compelled to commit a crime because of an immediate threat of death or serious bodily harm by another person. For a successful defence of duress, there has to have been an imminent peril and a direct connection between the threat and the offence charged (*R v Cole* [1994]).

In *R v Shaylor* [2001], the House of Lords recognised that the threat or threats could be directed towards the defendant, or a person or persons for whom he is responsible, but that it must cause them to be in fear of death or grievous bodily harm.

Availability

Since the courts want to encourage people to resist giving in to the pressures to commit crime, they have limited the availability of duress. In particular, the defence is not available in relation to murder or to an accomplice to murder (*R v Howe* [1987]) or in relation to attempted murder (*R v Gotts* [1991]). In addition, the defence is not available in relation to some forms of treason.

The defence of duress will not be available to a defendant if there is evidence that he had the opportunity to get help before the threat was due to be carried out, although regard will be had to his belief as to whether help could have been provided (*R v Hudson and Taylor* [1971]). A threat giving rise to duress can be imminent even though the threat is not one that is going to be carried out there and then (*R v Abdul-Hussain and Others* [1999]).

The defence is not available to those who **voluntarily** associate with criminals. In *R v Hasan* [2005], it was held that the defence should be denied 'when as a result of the accused's voluntary association with others engaged in criminal activity, he foresaw or ought reasonably to have foreseen the risk of being subjected to any compulsion by threats of violence.'

Onus of proof

If there are no facts from which the defence might reasonably be inferred in the prosecution's case, then the defendant has to produce some evidence of duress. Once this has been done, the onus of disproving duress rests on the prosecution.

The direction for duress

The direction to be given to the jury where the defendant raises the defence of duress is that laid down by the Court of Appeal in *R v Graham* [1982], as approved by the House of Lords in *R v Howe* [1987].

The jury should consider whether the defendant was compelled to act as he did because, on the basis of the circumstances as he honestly believed them to be, he thought his life was in immediate danger. If so, would a sober person of reasonable firmness sharing the defendant's characteristics have responded in the same way to the threats?

Two criteria need to be satisfied: the defendant must have honestly believed in the threat and the response must be one which would have been expected of the reasonable person.

This reasonableness test has been slightly modified so that the reasonable person can share some of the characteristics of the defendant. In *R v Bowen* [1996] the court held that the defendant's age, sex and a recognised psychiatric condition could all be relevant.

A characteristic of the accused of pliability or vulnerability which falls short of psychiatric illness is not a characteristic which can be attributed to the reasonable person for the purposes of the objective limb of the above test (*R v Horne* [1994]).

Coercion

Coercion is a special version of duress which is only available to a wife who commits an offence (other than treason or murder) in the presence of, and under the coercion of, her husband.

The defence appears to be somewhat broader than duress as it encompasses 'pressure' as well as threats of physical violence (*R v Richman* [1982]).

The Law Commission has long advocated reform of the law on duress. Its most recent report (2006) advocated that the focus on the reasonable person should be changed in favour of a focus upon the defendant's own ability to resist.

Duress: The Three Steps	[1] A threat or threats directed towards the defendant, or a person or persons for whom he is responsible …
	[2] Causing them to be in imminent fear of death or grievous bodily harm …
	[3] Provided that they honestly believed in the threat and the response must be one which would have been expected of the reasonable person

(7) SELF-DEFENCE

The common law allows the citizen to use reasonable force to protect his own person, his property and the person of another. In addition, s 3(1) of the Criminal Law Act 1967 permits the use of reasonable force in order to prevent crime or to arrest offenders.

Self-defence is similar to necessity and duress in the sense that the defendant will be faced with a choice of evils. The defendant will either commit a crime, perhaps homicide or a serious assault, or submit to harm being inflicted on himself, his property or the person of another.

However, unlike necessity and duress, self-defence or s 3(1) can constitute a defence to any crime, including murder and treason.

Reasonable force

There are two basic requirements:

First, the defendant must believe that the circumstances render it reasonable to use force for the purpose of crime prevention. This is an entirely subjective test.

Second, the force used by the defendant must be reasonable. This seems to be an objective test.

Only reasonable force may be used in self-defence, defence of property or another, crime prevention and lawful arrest. However, what is reasonable depends upon the circumstances; force which might be reasonable to prevent a violent attack upon the person could be unreasonable in relation to a less serious crime.

The Criminal Justice and Immigration Act 2008 s 76 clarifies that the second requirement has a subjective element. It states that the question of whether the force was reasonable in the circumstance is to be decided by reference to the circumstances that the defendant believed them to be, regardless of whether that belief was unreasonable or mistaken. This simply articulates the position that existed at common law (*R v Williams (Gladstone)* [1984]; *R v Owino* [1995]).

In *Re A (Children) (Conjoined twins: surgical separation)* [2001], Robert Walker LJ suggested that if a 6-year-old child firing a gun indiscriminately in a school playground was shot and killed by a defendant to prevent further harm, the defendant would be able to rely on the defence of self-defence at common law.

In assessing the reasonableness of the force used, the jury should be directed to take into account the defendant's physical characteristics but not those relating to his mental health (*R v Martin* [2002]).

(8) MISTAKE

Mistake of law

Ignorance of the criminal law is no defence: *R v Esop* [1836].

Ignorance of the civil law may exceptionally be a defence if it means that the defendant did not form the needed *mens rea*: *R v Smith DR* [1974].

> ### ▶ R v SMITH DR [1974]
>
> **Although a mistake of law is generally not a defence, a mistake as to the civil law may be a defence if it means that the defendant could not form the *mens rea* needed for the offence.**
>
> Facts
>
> A tenant was charged with criminal damage to certain fixtures in the flat. He thought that they were his own. However, as a matter of land law, as fixtures they belonged to the landlord.
>
> Held
>
> The court quashed his conviction on the grounds that he could not have had the needed *mens rea* to damage 'property belonging to another'.

Mistake of fact

A mistake of fact is a defence is relevant where it means that the prosecution cannot prove its case. Such mistakes are relevant in two situations. First where the mistake prevents the defendant from forming the *mens rea* for the crime in question. Second, where the mistake raises an excuse which means that the defendant should not be found liable even though the defendant has formed the *mens rea*.

The first situation applies where the defendant's mistake means that the *mens rea* of the offence cannot be formed. For example, if an individual, in a field, shoots a victim dead with a crossbow from a long distance, honestly believing he was firing at a scarecrow, the defendant would lack the necessary *mens rea* for murder, ie the intention to kill or cause grievous bodily harm (although he may be liable for other offences).

For offences where the *mens rea* is satisfied by intention only or by recklessness, it need only be shown that the defendant had an honest belief in the mistaken fact, which need not necessarily be a reasonable belief (*DPP v Morgan* [1975]). However, the more unreasonable the mistake the less likely the jury are to believe the mistake was genuine. Note that an honest belief in consent is no longer a defence to rape: a mistaken belief as to consent must now be reasonably held (s 1 Sexual Offences Act 2003).

Mistake can be a defence to crimes of negligence provided that the mistake is a reasonable one, since an unreasonable mistake itself supplies the negligence on which liability is based (*R v Tolson* [1889]). However, even a reasonable mistake is no defence to an offence of strict liability since the *mens rea* of the defendant is irrelevant in relation to one or more elements of the *actus reus* (*R v Prince* [1874]).

Mistakes of fact regarding defences

So far, we have only been concerned with mistakes of fact that mean that the defendant does not form the *mens rea* of the offence. As noted above, the other situation where a mistake of fact will be relevant is where the mistake raises an excuse which means that the defendant should not be found liable even though the defendant has formed the *mens rea*.

This typically applies where the defendant mistakenly thinks that they are entitled to a defence. They may think that they are acting under duress when they are not. The general rule is that such a mistake does not affect the *mens rea* of the crime. Therefore, the rule in *DPP v Morgan* [1975] does not apply. A mistake of fact will be relevant if it is both honest and reasonable (*R v Hasan* [2005]).

Mistakes about duress serve as an example of this. If the defendant mistakenly thinks that a third party has put him under duress and then commits a crime, then he still has formed the *mens rea* of that crime even though his actions were built on a mistake. As a result, the *DPP v Morgan* [1975] rule that a mistake need only be honest to be relevant does not apply. The defendant is only entitled to rely on his mistake of fact if it was both honest and reasonable.

However, mistakes about entitlement to self-defence provide an exception to this rule. Where a defendant mistakenly thinks that they are acting in self-defence, the mistake will be relevant if it is honest (*R v Williams (Gladstone)* [1984]). This is because such a mistake means that the defendant cannot form the *mens rea* of the crime. Since an assault requires the application of unlawful force, a defendant cannot be liable if he intended to apply lawful force. Since the mistake affects the *mens rea* of the crime, the rule in *DPP v Morgan* [1975] applies: the mistake needs only to be honest; there is no requirement that the mistake be reasonable. This is now articulated in statutory form in s 76(4) of the Criminal Justice and Immigration Act 2008.

Drunken mistakes about defences are always irrelevant. As we have seen, in relation to most defences (such as duress), a mistake will only be relevant if it is both honest and reasonable. This means that a drunken mistake will not be relevant because such a mistake will not be reasonable. The reasonable person would not be intoxicated.

Moreover, drunken mistakes about self-defence are treated in the same way as any other drunken mistake. As a matter of logic, drunken mistake as to self-defence should be relevant because such a mistake need not be reasonable. However, the courts have taken a different route. In *R v O'Grady* [1987] Lord Lane went against his own earlier reasoning in *Gladstone Williams* [1983] to hold that the mistake was irrelevant if it was induced by voluntary intoxication. This is now articulated in statutory form in s 76(5) of the Criminal Justice and Immigration Act 2008.

Mistake	When relevant	Authority
Mistake of criminal law	relevant	*R v Esop* [1836]
Mistake of civil law	Exceptionally relevant if it means that defendant could not form *mens rea*	*R v Smith DR* [1974]
Mistake of fact in relation to crimes requiring intention or recklessness	Relevant if honest (and means that the defendant could not form *mens rea*)	*DPP v Morgan* [1975]
Mistake of fact in relation to crimes requiring negligence	Relevant if honest and reasonable (and means that the defendant could not form *mens rea*)	*R v Tolson* [1889]
Mistake of fact in relation to crimes of strict liability	Not relevant	*R v Prince* [1874]
Mistake as to entitlement of a defence – such as duress	Relevant if honest and reasonable	*R v Hasan* [2005]
Mistake as to the entitlement of self-defence	Relevant if honest (and means that the defendant could not form *mens rea*)	*R v Williams (Gladstone)* [1984] Criminal Justice and Immigration Act 2008 s **76(4)**
Drunken mistake as to entitlement of any defence – including self-defence	Not relevant	*R v O'Grady* [1987]; Criminal Justice and Immigration Act 2008 s **76(5)** (in relation to self-defence)

You should now be confident that you would be able to tick all of the boxes on the checklist at the beginning of this chapter. To check your knowledge of General defences why not visit the companion website and take the Multiple Choice Question test. Check your understanding of the terms and vocabulary used in this chapter with the flashcard glossary.

Putting it into practice…

Now that you've mastered the basics, you will want to put it all into practice. The Routledge Questions and Answers series provides an ideal opportunity for you to apply your understanding and knowledge of the law and to hone your essay-writing technique.

We've included one exam-style essay question, which replicates the type of question posed in the Routledge Questions and Answers series to give you some essential exam practice. The Q&A includes an answer plan and a fully worked model answer to help you recognise what examiners might look for in your answer.

QUESTION 1

[For a practice to be subject to the criminal sanction] it is not enough in our submission that [it] is ... regarded as immoral. Nor is it enough that it should cause harm. Both of these are minimal conditions for action by means of the criminal law, but they are not sufficient.

Clarkson, CMV and Keating, HM,
Criminal Law: Text and Materials,
London: Sweet & Maxwell, 1990, p 25

Discuss.

Answer plan

The quotation expresses the commonly held view that immorality and harmfulness are necessary but not sufficient conditions of criminal liability; that the legislator ought to consider further matters when deciding whether to criminalise or legalise particular conduct. The starting point in answering this question is the well known 'debate' of the 1950s and 1960s between Lord Devlin and Professor Hart:

- the 'moral' theory: the Wolfenden Committee and Lord Devlin's response to the Report;

- criticisms of the 'moral' theory – its irrationalism;

- the 'harm' principle;

- the limitations of the 'harm' principle;

136

- considerations additional to the supposed immorality or harmfulness of the behaviour – the social effects of prohibition and enforcement;

- is immorality a 'necessary' condition?

ANSWER

In 1959, Lord Devlin delivered the Maccabean Lecture in Jurisprudence of the British Academy under the title 'The enforcement of morals', in which he argued that the legislature is entitled to use the criminal law against behaviour which is generally condemned as immoral.

The catalyst for Lord Devlin's thesis was the *Report of the Wolfenden Committee on Homosexual Offences and Prostitution*, 1957. The Committee had recommended that homosexual behaviour between consenting adults in private should no longer be a criminal offence. The Committee thought it was not the function of the law to intervene in the private lives of citizens or to enforce any particular morality except where it is necessary to protect the citizen from what is offensive or injurious and to provide protection against exploitation and corruption.

Lord Devlin disagreed. He contended that there are no limits to the power of the State to legislate against immoral behaviour: 'immorality' is a necessary and sufficient condition of criminalisation.

He based his argument upon the premise that social harmony is jeopardised if morality is not underwritten by the law. According to this view, tolerance of immorality threatens the social fabric, and therefore the legislature should criminalise behaviour where it is clear that there is a 'collective judgment' condemning the behaviour in question. Lord Devlin argued that morality forms a 'seamless web'. By this metaphor, he intended to convey the notion that 'society's morals' form a fragile structure and that if morality is not generally reinforced by legal means, then damage to the entire structure will follow.

According to Lord Devlin, immorality is what every 'right-minded' person considers to be immoral. If the behaviour in question provokes feelings of disgust and indignation in this 'individual', then it should be subject to the criminal sanction. Lord Devlin suggested that the judiciary are particularly well placed to express the appropriate standards by virtue of their familiarity with the 'reasonable man in the jury'.

There are a number of objections to Lord Devlin's thesis; the principal criticisms relate to its rejection of rationality. Instead of rational argument and empirical investigation of the effects of criminalisation or legalisation, Lord Devlin advocated that we place our reliance upon presumptions about the feelings of the right-minded individual and assumptions about the societal effects of liberalisation and tolerance.

Opponents of Devlin's thesis argue that although the feelings of the community are an important consideration, they cannot be the sole basis for deciding whether behaviour is to be subject to the criminal sanction, and if the revulsion of the ordinary person is a dangerous basis for criminalisation, then reliance on judicial estimates of that disgust is even more dangerous. Bentham warned us to be suspicious when officials claim that they are acting in the name of 'right-minded people'. In many cases, 'popular opinion' is used as a pretext to justify the prejudices of the legislators themselves (*Theory of Legislation*, 1876).

With reference to Lord Devlin's assertion that morality forms a seamless web, Professor Hart claimed in *Immorality and Treason* (1959) that there is no evidence that people abandon their moral views about murder, cruelty and dishonesty purely because a practice which they regard as immoral is not punished by law.

He argued that the proper approach to determining whether the criminal law should intervene involves full consideration of the social consequences of the conduct in question. To this extent, he advocated the liberal approach, which stresses the importance of rational analysis in terms of the possible harmful consequences of the conduct. The principle of democracy may require the legislator to consider the values of the 'moral majority', but the liberal tradition urges that the autonomy of the individual be respected and that individuals have rights that may trump majority preferences. Professor Hart argued that a reasoned assessment of the harmful effects of the behaviour is a far better approach to the question of whether it should be outlawed than simple reliance on the feelings of disgust that the behaviour might cause us to feel.

The general approach of this tradition was expressed by John Stuart Mill in his essay, *On Liberty*. He maintained that the exercise of force over an individual is justified only if it is done to prevent harm to others. The fact that the behaviour might cause harm to the person who performs it is no justification for criminalisation.

Harm, however, is not to be understood as restricted to 'physical harm', but to include the violation of any recognised interest (Gross, H, *A Theory of Criminal Justice*, Oxford: OUP, 1979). Professor Hart contended that cruelty to animals should be outlawed, although there is no harm caused to other people. In addition, legal intervention may be appropriate to restrain young people from certain activities. This is justified not on the grounds that the behaviour may cause harm to the young person, but on the grounds that such a person is not sufficiently mature to appreciate the dangers of the behaviour in question.

It might be supposed that harm theorists would be opposed to legislation controlling narcotics or compelling the use of seat belts in motor vehicles, on the basis that legislation of this type involves a violation of the fundamental principle of individual autonomy. The harm theorist is opposed to legislation designed to protect the individual from himself.

In fact, legislation of this type is often supported by modern harm theorists. They point out that the prohibited behaviour is potentially harmful to others. In 'The role of law in drug control', Kaplan explains that there are different categories of harm, any one of which may be used to justify the criminalisation of behaviour that at first sight appears only to expose the actor to the risk of harm. The individual who drives a car without wearing a seat belt or the person who consumes drugs may expose others to a 'public ward harm'. That is, he may impose on others the cost of rectifying the damage he causes himself. He may be rendered incapable of discharging economic responsibilities he owes to others ('non-support harm'). Alternatively, a case may be made out that if the individual is allowed to indulge in certain behaviour, other susceptible individuals may copy or 'model' the behaviour and suffer harm as a consequence.

This reveals one of the limitations of the liberal 'harm' theory. When secondary harms are taken into account, the theory appears to lack precision. As Kaplan points out, if we acknowledge the broad concept of harm, there are few actions that one can perform that threaten harm only to oneself.

Moreover, the prohibition of particular harmful conduct may, in itself, result in harmful consequences. For example, the sale of certain commodities (heroin, alcohol, sugar, petrol, hamburgers, etc.) may directly or indirectly cause physical harm to consumers. However, prohibiting the sale of those commodities will cause economic harm to the business enterprises involved, and so we must weigh the harms resulting from tolerance against the harms of prohibition.

In *Principles of Morals and Legislation* (1781), Bentham recognised that in this process, careful consideration should be given to the general effects of prohibition. Even though certain behaviour may be regarded as immoral or harmful, it should not be prohibited if punishment would be inefficacious as a deterrent or the harm caused by prohibition would be greater than that which would be suffered if the behaviour was left unpunished.

For example, it is sometimes argued that as the demand for certain commodities and services (for example, prostitution, abortion, alcohol and other drugs) is relatively inelastic, there is little point in criminalisation of the behaviour concerned. Indeed, it is suggested that criminalisation may make matters worse. Prior to legalisation, backstreet abortions were carried out in conditions of great risk to the mother. Legalisation permits official control, allowing matters of public health to be addressed. Similarly, if prostitution were decriminalised, one condition of operating as a licensed or registered prostitute might be periodic health checks.

In addition, the criminalisation of certain types of conduct (for example, the possession of drugs) requires, for reasons of enforcement, intrusive forms of policing, involving, for example, powers of stop and search. There is the danger that these powers might be used in a discriminatory and oppressive manner against particular groups. The outlawing of homosexual behaviour meant that the police were often involved in dubious and degrading practices to catch offenders.

Thus, the fact that behaviour is harmful to others cannot be a sufficient condition of prohibition. The virtue of the harm theory is that, at least, it focuses attention on the empirical issues concerning the social effects of the conduct and the effects of legal intervention – issues which the moral principle patently ignores.

The quotation suggests that immorality is a necessary condition of criminalisation. Is this correct? What importance should be attached to the moral feelings of a section of the community?

It is sometimes argued that support for the law is stronger where the prohibited conduct is perceived by a significant section of the population to be immoral. It is submitted, however, that immorality ought not to be regarded as a necessary condition of prohibition. Much of modern criminal legislation (for example, road traffic laws) is concerned with conduct which would not ordinarily be termed 'immoral', but one would be hard-pressed to deny the need for that legislation.

In any case, where behaviour is perceived to be immoral, it is normally supported by empirical claims expressed in terms of the harmful consequences, real or imagined, that will result if the behaviour is tolerated. For example, Lord Devlin believed that tolerance of homosexuality would result in harm – that is, damage to society at large. If this hypothesis were testable, and if there were empirical evidence in its support, it would provide a very good argument in favour of prohibiting homosexuality.[1] On the other hand, the assertion that 'homosexuality should be prohibited because it is immoral' cannot be evaluated in the same way.

It is right that the debate should be focused on empirical claims. It is only by insisting upon arguments articulated in terms of the social consequences of tolerance, on the one hand, and prohibition, on the other, that a rational analysis of the fairness of legal intervention can be conducted.

The fact that a section of the community feels that certain behaviour is immoral cannot be either a necessary or a sufficient condition of prohibition. Although it may be prudent on some occasions for the legislator to acknowledge the 'feelings' of a section of the community – to ignore those irrational sentiments may result in the harmful consequence of social unrest – he should not rely upon the 'stomach of the man in the street'. Disgust or revulsion ought never to replace careful investigation of the social effects of prohibition.

Think point

1   Emperor Justinian believed that homosexual behaviour was the cause of earthquakes.